The Difference
Jesus Makes

The Difference Jesus Makes

Trusting Him in Every Situation

H. B. CHARLES JR.

MOODY PUBLISHERS

CHICAGO

All Scripture quotations, unless otherwise indicated, are taken from *The Holy Bible, English Standard Version.* Copyright © 2000, 2001 by Crossway Bibles, a division of Good News Publishers. Used by permission. All rights reserved.

Scripture quotations marked NIV are taken from the Holy Bible, New International Version®, NIV®. Copyright © 1973, 1978, 1984, 2011 by Biblica, Inc.™ Used by permission of Zondervan. All rights reserved worldwide. www.zondervan.com. The "NIV" and "New International Version" are trademarks registered in the United States Patent and Trademark Office by Biblica, Inc.™

Edited by Jim Vincent
Interior design: Smartt Guys design and Erik M. Peterson
Cover design: Geoff Sciacca and Erik M. Peterson
Cover image: Wavebreak Media / 123 RF
Author photo: Derrick Wilson

Library of Congress Cataloging-in-Publication Data

Charles, H. B.
  The difference Jesus makes : trusting Him in every situation / H.B. Charles Jr.
    pages cm
  ISBN 978-0-8024-1227-0
  1. Trust in God—Christianity. 2. Bible, Mark IV-V—Criticism, interpretation, etc. 3. Jesus Christ—Parables. I. Title.
  BV4637.C427 2014
  248.8'6--dc23

                                                         2014011023

We hope you enjoy this book from Moody Publishers. Our goal is to provide high-quality, thought-provoking books and products that connect truth to your real needs and challenges. For more information on other books and products written and produced from a biblical perspective, go to www.moodypublishers.com or write to:

Moody Publishers
820 N. LaSalle Boulevard
Chicago, IL 60610

3 5 7 9 10 8 6 4

Printed in the United States of America

To my wife, Crystal.

*The Lord Jesus Christ
has made all the difference in my life.
But one of the ways in which Christ
has changed me is by giving you to me.
I am who I am and where I am because of
your love, support, and encouragement.
You are my best friend, my ministry partner,
and my sunshine!
I love you.*

Contents

He Can Make
the Difference

I was in junior high school the first time a girl gave me her phone number. I did not ask for the number. As our families had dinner together that Sunday evening, it was obvious that I liked her. But I did not have the guts to ask for her number. I didn't even know that was what you were supposed to do. But she saved the day. Before we left the restaurant, the young lady told me she needed a pen. I borrowed one from somebody and gave it to her. She then wrote her number on a piece of paper, folded it, and handed it to me.

"Call me sometime," she said.

I was so blown away by what just happened, I didn't respond. But I had every intention of calling her. There was more important business, however, for me to tend to first.

I was the preacher's kid. And there was nothing "cool" about me back then (or now, for that matter). I hung out with the two most popular boys in school. But I was only popular because I hung out with Billy and Michael. We made an unbeatable team for three-on-three games at lunch. They were able to capitalize on our schoolyard "fame." The girls loved Billy and Michael. I, on the other hand, made the girls nervous when I came around. But I now had chips to get into the big game. I finally had a girl's phone number.

I didn't have a sense of fashion back then (or now, for that matter). If it was clean and did not itch, that's what I put on. But that Sunday night, I laid out my clothes. I ironed my pants and shirt. And when everything was in place, I put the folded paper with the girl's number in my back pocket.

The next day, at just the right time, I reached into my pocket and pulled out the number. "What's this?" I asked. "Oh, yeah. This is that girl's phone number. I forgot I had it."

You would have thought I just did a mesmerizing magic trick. The guys all gathered around and began to ooh and aah. They asked me questions about the girl. They asked me when I got the number. They had all kinds of questions. And I joyfully answered them all. It was great, so great that I couldn't let this be a one-time show. But I knew I would not be getting another girl's number any time soon. So I had to milk this situation for all it was worth. I kept the number in my pocket for days. And whenever I had a new audience, I would go through my routine. It wowed the crowd every time.

Eventually, the multiple shows took their toll on my key prop.

The folded piece of paper ripped. But I refused to let that end my performance. I simply got another piece of paper and wrote the girl's number on it. And the show continued. But it was just a show. I impressed all the guys in school with a number that I never used. The pretty young lady who gave it to me was a year older than I. But my father said she was too "mature" for me. So he did not allow me to talk to her. In fact, I was not allowed to talk to any girls on the phone at the time. Dad said I wasn't ready. I had been strutting around the schoolyard for days bragging about a number from a person I had no relationship with.

I can look back at my boyhood shenanigans and laugh. But that experience also troubles me. I don't want that to be my experience with Jesus.

The Lord Jesus Christ has reached out to us in His incarnation, taking on flesh and becoming one of us. And He has given us His "number," if you will. He has given us the Word of God by which we can know Him better. Many of us carry it around with us. We bring it up in conversation to impress others. But we do not have a real, life-changing relationship with Jesus. Is that you? Are you professing something you do not possess? Have you experienced the difference Jesus makes?

The goal of this book is to show you from the Word of God that Jesus is worthy of your trust in every situation. No matter what is going on in your life, Jesus can make the difference.

I endeavor to press this case by retelling a series of miracles Jesus performed, as recorded in the gospel of Mark (chapters 2, 4–5). Most of these miracles follow a long day of ministry, in which

Jesus taught the crowds the parables of the kingdom of heaven (Mark 4:1–33). These parables affirm that Jesus is the Messiah-King, the fulfillment of Old Testament prophecies and promises. And these parables assert the certainty of the kingdom of heaven, regardless of how things in the world may look to the unbelieving eye.

These parables of the kingdom teach us to look to Jesus for the truth. We are constantly bombarded by bad news. But in Jesus there is news from another network in heaven. It is good news. It is the message of the gospel that declares the scandalous grace of God, who sent His only Son into the world to redeem rebellious sinners like you and me. This news is only found in Jesus. "I am the way, and the truth, and the life," said Jesus. "No one comes to the Father except through me" (John 14:6).

Jesus is the truth. But the truth of Jesus is affirmed by the power He displayed. Peter pointed an unbelieving crowd to "Jesus of Nazareth, a man attested to you by God with mighty works and wonders and signs that God did through him in your midst, as you yourselves know" (Acts 2:22). God the Father testified to the life, ministry, and message of Jesus by the mighty works He performed.

Truth and power work together to affirm the identity of Jesus. And we need to experience both. We need to read and hear and study the message of Christ. But we also need to experience the life-changing power Jesus works for those who trust in Him. No, I am not suggesting that you should expect a miracle in your life. I believe in the sovereignty of God to intervene in our circumstances, even in miraculous ways. No, I do not believe that miracles are normative today. The miracles we will study are not meant to bid you to expect Jesus to do the same thing in your life. But may this study give you confidence that the Lord is able to make a difference in your life in every situation. The Lord may not choose to do it the way you expect. But He has everything under control. And He is worthy of your trust today.

One day, a little boy sat staring at a picture on the wall. In the frame was a picture of his father, who had been away on military duty for some time. The boy's mother was not alarmed by his extended period of quiet gazing. This was the boy's typical routine to deal with his father's absence. But she rushed to the room this time, as she heard her son sobbing. She grabbed him in her arms and tried to wipe his tears away, even as the tears continued to flow. Finally, he calmed down, and she asked what the matter was.

"I want my daddy to come out of the frame," he replied.

Have you ever felt like that in your relationship with God? Sure, you've read about the love, power, and goodness of God in the great stories of the Bible. Yet when it comes to the challenges you face, it seems that God is in a frame, as it were. You feel like the Lord is disconnected from the circumstances you face. We want God to come out of the frame!

This is what God has done in the person of the Lord Jesus Christ. In the incarnation, God stepped out of the frame. He took on human flesh. He became one of us. He sweated in our heat and shivered in our cold. The Lord shared our experience in order to sympathize with us in our weaknesses (Hebrews 4:15).

But in Jesus we have more than a divine sympathy. We have divine strength. He cares about what you are going through. So do others in your life who love you and are concerned about your situation. But Jesus cares perfectly. And, moreover, He is able to make the difference in your life.

In the Gospels, we meet Jesus the teacher and preacher. He proclaimed the truth of the kingdom of heaven. But we also meet Jesus the miracle worker. The miracles of Jesus affirm the truth of His message. But there is another important message in the miracles of Jesus that is not to be ignored. Jesus is able to make the difference in your life, no matter what you are dealing with.

You can trust Jesus when you have overwhelming needs and limited resources.

You can trust Jesus when you are engulfed in a raging storm.

You can trust Jesus when you are bound by evil that will not let you go.

You can trust Jesus when the doctors announce they have done everything they can do to help you.

You can trust Jesus when you are facing a dead end crowded with impossibility.

You can trust Jesus when you have overwhelming needs and limited resources.

Jesus is able to make the difference in your life. You must trust Him. But that's the simple part. He has proven over and over again that He is worthy of your trust. Bring the burdens of your life to Him. And then stand back and watch Him make the difference!

And when he returned to Capernaum after some days, it was reported that
he was at home. And many were gathered together, so that there was no
more room, not even at the door. And he was preaching the word to them.
And they came, bringing to him a paralytic carried by four men. And when
they could not get near him because of the crowd, they removed the roof
above him, and when they had made an opening, they let down the bed
on which the paralytic lay. And when Jesus saw their faith, he said to the
paralytic, "Son, your sins are forgiven." Now some of the scribes were sitting there, questioning in their hearts, "Why does this man speak like that?
He is blaspheming! Who can forgive sins but God alone?" And immediately
Jesus, perceiving in his spirit that they thus questioned within themselves,
said to them, "Why do you question these things in your hearts? Which is
easier, to say to the paralytic, 'Your sins are forgiven,' or to say, 'Rise, take
up your bed and walk'? But that you may know that the Son of Man has
authority on earth to forgive sins"—he said to the paralytic—"I say to you,
rise, pick up your bed, and go home." And he rose and immediately picked
up his bed and went out before them all, so that they were all amazed and
glorified God, saying, "We never saw anything like this!"

MARK 2:1–12

CHAPTER 1

Embracing the
Priorities of Jesus

The miracles brought the crowds to Jesus, but they distracted from the teaching ministry of Jesus. The carpenter's son, now Himself a carpenter turned teaching rabbi, had been born in Bethlehem and raised in Nazareth. But Capernaum was His home and headquarters during His Galilean ministry. Simon Peter, one of the initial disciples, also lived in Capernaum. Here, Mark tells us, Jesus healed the sick—including Simon Peter's mother-in-law—and cast out demons.

The people wanted more miracles, but Jesus knew His mission was to teach about the kingdom of God. So He left Capernaum to preach and teach in the neighboring cities along the northern shore of the Sea of Galilee.

Now Jesus had returned to Capernaum. And the news spread

quickly that He was at home. When they found out where Jesus was, they packed the house (Mark 2:1–2). There was standing room only. People huddled around the doors and windows to see and hear Jesus.

THE MIXED MOTIVES OF THE CROWD

But not everyone was there for the right reasons. Some were there because they believed Jesus to be the long-awaited Messiah-King. Others were not sure and wanted further evidence. Still others were just there to see the wonder worker do His thing. Verse 6 tells us the scribes were there. Luke 5:17 adds the Pharisees were also present. They hoped to catch Jesus saying or doing something they could use to discredit Him.

These competing motivations of the crowd did not move Jesus. The main thing is to keep the main thing the main thing. Yet the last thing many us know is what to put first. And we are prone to impose our mixed-up priorities on Jesus. But the priorities of Jesus will not and cannot change. Jesus always prioritizes the eternal over the temporary.

A cathedral in Italy has three entrances, each next to the other and each having an inscription above it. Over the left entrance is written the words, "All that pleases is but for a moment." Over the right entrance is inscribed, "All that troubles is but for a moment." In the center is the larger main entrance over which is the statement: "Nothing is important except that which is eternal." That simple statement is a profound truth.

Now, here's some good news and bad news. The good news is

your bad days will not last forever. The bad news is your good days will not last forever. All that pleases and troubles is but for a moment. Nothing is important except that which is eternal. Jesus always prioritizes the eternal over the temporary. And the priorities of Jesus are to be the priorities of every Christian, every church. Mark 2:1–12 affirms the priorities of Jesus in four movements.

Mark reports that after the people learned that Jesus "was at home . . . many were gathered together, so that there was no more room, not even at the door" (vv. 1–2). This is the way it ought to be. The presence of Jesus ought to be our drawing card. Unfortunately, the church often tries to draw people by unworthy means. Church advertisements spotlight charismatic preachers, excellent music, multiple programs, impressive facilities, and fun activities without mentioning Jesus. These things may have their place. But if Jesus is not obviously present and actively in charge, people will not experience transforming grace.

Nothing we do in church matters if it is not about Jesus. Let me state what the church should be about in five words: Jesus only and only Jesus. In John 12:32, Jesus said, "And I, when I am lifted up from the earth, will draw all people to myself." May this be the report published about every church: Jesus is here!

JESUS' RESPONSE TO THE CROWD

How did Jesus respond to the presence of the crowd? The end of verse 2 says, "And he was preaching the word to them." Jesus did not put on a show for the crowd. Indeed, there were those who were there to be entertained by the wonders Jesus performed. And by the time the crowd left, "they were all amazed" (v. 12). But that was not Jesus' agenda. Jesus wanted those who were present to glorify God and to enjoy Him forever. So Jesus preached the Word to them.

In Mark 1, Jesus healed the sick and cast out demons. Then He went to a desolate place to pray. Simon and the others hunted Him down. When they found Him, they said, "Everyone is looking for you" (1:37). The name of Jesus had become prominent. The works of Jesus had become publicized. And the ministry of Jesus had become popular. Jesus should have struck while the iron was hot, built on His momentum, and taken advantage of the opportunity. Instead, Jesus wandered off into the wilderness to pray.

Simon and the boys were dumbfounded. "Everyone is looking for you," they said. "Where have you been? What are you doing? Why are you letting this opportunity slip away?" Jesus answered, "Let us go on to the next towns, that I may preach there also, for that is why I came out" (v. 38). The priorities of Jesus were exercised through biblical preaching.

I love music. I live and work with an ongoing soundtrack of Christian music in my mind and heart. And I am looking forward to heaven where there will be no pulpits, only choir stands. But if that heavenly choir stand is to be populated with redeemed voices in praise to God, the church on earth must preach the Word. Unfortunately, many pastors and churches have jettisoned the centrality of biblical preaching. Ours is the day described in 2 Timothy 4:3–4: "For the time is coming when people will not endure sound teaching, but having itching ears they will accumulate for themselves teachers to suit their own passions, and will turn away from listening to the truth and wander off into myths." But it is still the will of God to save the lost and sanctify the church through doctrinally sound, Christ-centered, and Spirit-empowered proclamation of the Scriptures.

The apostle Paul wrote, "For 'everyone who calls on the name of the Lord will be saved.'" (Romans 10:13) Then he explained why the spiritually lost do not call on the Lord for salvation: "How then will they call on him in whom they have not believed? And how are they to believe in him of whom they have never heard? And how are they to hear without someone preaching?" (verses 14–15). If lives are to be changed for eternity, someone has to preach the Word.

JESUS' RESPONSE TO THE
FAITH OF THE STRETCHER-BEARERS

After setting the scene, Mark plunges us into the drama with the actions of the stretcher-bearers and the reaction of Jesus.

As Jesus was preaching the Word to this packed house, five nameless men arrived. One was a paralytic. Was he born this way? Did he become paralyzed by some tragic event? Was his paralysis the result of sin? We are not told. The text only tells us that four men carried this invalid to Jesus. We know a couple of things about these four who brought this paralyzed man to Jesus.

First, these stretcher-bearers loved their friend. The text does not call them friends. But their actions make it clear they had a special relationship to this paralytic. They carried him to Jesus. In our day, a person with paralysis can live with relative independence. That was not the case in Jesus' day. Without assistance, a paralytic was helpless. John 5 records the story of a man crippled for thirty-eight years who lay by the pool called Bethesda. No one would help him into the pool. But this paralytic had four friends who cared enough to help him overcome his condition. In Acts 3, another crippled man was laid at the temple's Beautiful Gate to beg for money from the worshipers. But did they try to get him help beyond the gate? These stretcher-bearers loved their friend so much that they took him to Jesus for healing.

Second, *these stretcher-bearers believed in Jesus*. Verse 4 says, "And when they could not get near him because of the crowd, they removed the roof above him, and when they had made an opening, they let down the bed on which the paralytic lay." The houses had flat roofs made of wood planks covered with branches, thatch, and mud. Accessed by ladder, these roofs were used like patio decks. The stretcher-bearers carried the paralytic up the ladder, dug through the roof, and lowered the paralytic to Jesus' feet. They were determined to get him to Jesus. The presence of the crowd could not stop them. The potential anger of the homeowner could not stop them. The possibility of rebuke from Jesus could not stop them. Their friend had a need only Jesus could meet. They had to get him to Jesus.

Scripture emphasizes that faith is seen more than it is heard. James 2:17 says, "Faith by itself, if it does not have works, is dead."

Do you have loved ones whose lives are in paralysis? It may not be physical. But they are nonetheless crippled, impaired, and broken. Do you believe

Jesus can help them? Then grab your end of the stretcher. Tear up the roof. Do whatever it takes to get them to Jesus.

Preachers do not like their sermons interrupted. But Jesus did not get angry when these men interrupted His message to lower the paralytic to Him. Instead, He "saw their faith" (v. 5). This reference to faith may include the paralytic, but it focuses on the stretcher-bearers. Jesus saw their faith. It was evidenced by what they did, not by anything they said. There is a popular but false teaching that claims faith-filled words create reality. But Scripture emphasizes that faith is seen more than it is heard. The profession of faith does not assume the possession of faith. James 2:17 says, "So also faith by itself, if it does not have works, is dead."

These stretcher-bearers had living faith. Even if the paralytic didn't believe, they did. Verse 5 says when Jesus saw their faith, he addressed the paralytic. Jesus addressed him as "Son." This is not a statement about his age. It is a term of endearment. Jesus cared about the man like a loving father cares for a troubled son.

After that tender word, Jesus addressed the man with targeted words: "Son, your sins are forgiven." The stretcher-bearers brought this paralytic to Jesus for healing, not forgiveness. This is the danger of coming to Jesus. He may give you what you need rather than what you want. Jesus is not preoccupied with felt needs. His priority is to minister to your biggest problem, which is not your physical condition, financial situation, or relationship status.

Our biggest problem is that God is holy and we are not. And we will have to answer to God for how we have lived our lives.

The Scriptures declare, "'None is righteous, no, not one; no one understands; no one seeks for God. All have turned aside; together they have become worthless; no one does good, not even one'" (Romans 3:10–12). We are guilty sinners with no righteous merit to commend for divine approval.

We cannot reach up to God, but God has reached down to us through the death and resurrection of Christ. Jesus came to solve your biggest problem by providing forgiveness of sins at the cross. As Warren Wiersbe wrote: "Forgiveness is the greatest miracle Jesus ever performs. It meets the greatest need; it costs the greatest price; and it brings the greatest blessings and the most lasting results."[1]

JESUS' RESPONSE
TO THE CRITICISMS OF THE SCRIBES

Mark does not tell us how the paralytic or the stretcher-bearers responded to Jesus' announcement of forgiveness. He instead turns his attention to the scribes, the theological scholars of the day. When they heard Jesus declare the paralytic's sins forgiven, they began "questioning in their hearts" (v. 6). When we speak of the "heart" metaphorically, we refer to the emotions. But in Scripture, the "heart" symbolizes the intellect more than the emotions. The words of Jesus did not make the scribes feel a certain way as much as it caused them to draw negative conclusions about Jesus. "Why does this man speak like that?" they asked with contempt. "He is blaspheming! Who can forgive sins but God alone?" (v. 7).

These are damning indictments. As Christians, we do not agree with them. But we can affirm the formula they used to reach their conclusion. The scribes asked, "Who can forgive sins but God alone?" The assumed answer to this rhetorical question is no one. The priests could declare a person's sins forgiven after he offered proper sacrifices and demonstrated genuine repentance. But the priests only ratified what God had done. True forgiveness comes only from God. Isaiah 43:25 says, "I, I am he who blots out your transgressions for my own sake, and I will not remember your sins." Forgiveness is God's business. And He does not have any staff or partners or coworkers in His business.

The scribes were right. No one can forgive sins but God alone. But the verdict they rendered was wrong. They declared, "He is blasphem-ing!" Blasphemy is impious or irreverent speech toward God. It is to talk in a way that brings God down to your level or lifts you up to God's level. Leviticus 24:16 says, "Whoever blasphemes the name of the Lord shall surely be put to death." This is the crime for which Jesus was crucified. During His trial, the high priest asked if

> **Anyone who reads the Gospels and concludes Jesus never claimed to be God can stare at a cloudless sky at high noon and never see the sun.**

He was the Christ, the Son of the Blessed? In Mark 14:62, Jesus answered: "I am, and you will see the Son of Man seated at the right hand of Power, and coming with the clouds of heaven." When the high priest heard this, he tore his garments and asked what more evidence was needed against Jesus. And they all condemned Him as deserving death. In our text, the scribes were convinced they had evidence against Jesus. In announcing this paralytic's sins forgiven, Jesus was claiming the divine authority.

There are those who contend the deity of Jesus is the theological construct of revisionist Christianity—that the early church concocted this theory to boost their fledgling movement. Jesus never claimed to be God, they say, and would be embarrassed by the suggestion. But anyone who reads the Gospels and concludes Jesus never claimed to be God can stare at a cloudless sky at high noon and never see the sun. If the crowd did not know what Jesus was saying, the scribes did. Their stubborn unbelief did not allow them to believe in Jesus. But at least they had the theological integrity to draw the lines at the right places. Either Jesus is God or He is a blasphemer. There is no middle ground. It does not suffice to say Jesus was a mighty prophet or a good teacher or a moral example. If Jesus was not God, He was a fraud who deserved to die on the cross for His sins. This was the conclusion of the scribes. "He is blaspheming," they said.

Jesus demonstrated His deity by responding to the unexpressed questions the scribes asked in their hearts. Jesus did not merely read their expressions. He saw their hearts. That is divine omniscience. Omniscience means that God knows everything—known, unknown, and knowable. Matthew Henry said, "God not only sees men, he sees through them." Jesus knew what the scribes were asking in their hearts. He answered their question with a question: "Why do you question these things in your hearts? Which is easier, to say to the paralytic, 'Your sins are forgiven,' or to say, 'Rise, take up your bed and walk'?" (vv. 8–9). This was a trick question. On one hand, it was easier for Jesus to say, "Your sins are forgiven." Because forgiveness is a spiritual issue, no one could verify if Jesus truly forgave his sins. On the other hand, it was easier for Jesus to say, "Rise, take up your bed and walk." Jesus could heal him by cash but He would have to forgive him on credit. Jesus would have to pay for that forgiveness at the cross.

The scribes thought they caught Jesus. But Jesus trapped them. Either answer would have affirmed Jesus before the crowd. No mere man can heal sickness or forgive sins. *Only God can heal sickness.* If you are sick, take advantage of the skill of doctors, the benefits of surgery, and the power of medicine. But do not put your hope in the hospital. Doctors only practice medicine. They do not perform miracles. Only God can heal sickness.

Likewise, *only God can forgive sins.* In Psalm 51:4, David confesses, "Against you, you only, have I sinned and done what is evil in your sight." For the record, David sinned against a lot of people. But ultimately he was right. All sin is committed against God. It does not mean anything to get it right with those you have offended if you do not get it right with God. In the sense of removing guilt, no human can forgive sins and you cannot forgive yourself. Only God forgives sins. Jesus declared His true identity to the religious establishment by confronting them with the fact that only God can heal sickness and forgive sins.

JESUS' RESPONSE TO THE NEED OF THE PARALYTIC

In verses 10–11, Jesus says, "'But that you may know that the Son of Man has authority on earth to forgive sins'—he said to the

paralytic—'I say to you, rise, pick up your bed, and go home.'"
This is the first of fourteen times the title "Son of Man" appears in
Mark. Mark 1:1 says, "The beginning of the gospel of Jesus Christ,
the Son of God." This is the most important title ascribed to Jesus.
Yet Jesus refers to Himself as the Son of Man. It may be that He
used this self-description for its ambiguity. It can refer to humanity or deity. It can be a human being or a supernatural being. It can
express humility or authority. Jesus could be calling Himself a man
or "The Man." The hearer had to choose. But Jesus clearly uses the
title here to state His divine authority: "that you may know that the
Son of Man has authority on earth to forgive sins."

Earlier, Jesus had granted the paralytic forgiveness of his sins
(v. 5). Now Jesus gives assurance of forgiveness. We need both.
Guilt will burden you down without forgiveness and assurance.
In his commentary on this passage, R. C. Sproul writes of being
offered a handsome salary to join a psychiatric clinic. Sproul confessed he did not know anything about psychiatrics. But his friend
rebutted that many people who came to his clinic needed a minister, not a psychiatrist.[2] Indeed, there are many people suffering
from mental, physical, and emotional problems that are rooted in
unresolved guilt. They need to know their sins have been forgiven.
Only Jesus can do that. And Jesus proved it by saying to the paralytic, "I say to you, rise, pick up your bed, and go home."

Verse 12 says the paralytic "rose and immediately picked up his
bed and went out before them all." This crippled man was lowered
through the roof on his bed. But when Jesus told him to arise, he
immediately stood up. He folded his cot and began to carry the

thing that had been carrying him. And the crowd that saw the paralytic dropped in saw him walk out. Their reaction? "They were all amazed." (v. 12). Their minds were blown. They knew this was a God thing. So they "glorified" God. Their worship was expressed in grateful praise. They said, "We never saw anything like this!" This is why we worship Jesus. There is no one like Him.

There is no door that Jesus cannot open.

There is no enemy that Jesus cannot defeat.

There is no need that Jesus cannot meet.

There is no pain that Jesus cannot comfort.

There is no problem that Jesus cannot solve.

There is no sickness that Jesus cannot heal.

There is no sin Jesus cannot forgive.

Jesus is still able to do amazing things you have never seen before. How do I know? On Good Friday, He died on the cross for sin. On Easter, He rose from the dead with the keys to death, hell, and the grave. And "He is able to save completely those who come to God through him, because he always lives" to make intercession for them (Hebrews 7:25 NIV).

On that day, when evening had come, he said to them, "Let us go across to the other side." And leaving the crowd, they took him with them in the boat, just as he was. And other boats were with him. And a great windstorm arose, and the waves were breaking into the boat, so that the boat was already filling. But he was in the stern, asleep on the cushion. And they woke him and said to him, "Teacher, do you not care that we are perishing?" And he awoke and rebuked the wind and said to the sea, "Peace! Be still!" And the wind ceased, and there was a great calm. He said to them, "Why are you so afraid? Have you still no faith?" And they were filled with great fear and said to one another, "Who then is this, that even the wind and the sea obey him?"

MARK 4:35–41

CHAPTER 2

Trusting Jesus
in a Storm

I remember my family's first visit to Jacksonville, Florida. The hot summer days caused us to take refuge in the hotel pool as much as possible. But one particular afternoon, our fun at the pool ended abruptly. Pointing to the sky, I said to my wife, "Look, Crystal! The storm clouds are rolling."

Having grown up in church, we both had heard many gospel songs about "storm clouds rolling in." But we had never seen it happen. We had a good laugh about it. But as we were joking around, the clouds were quickly moving over us. The blue sky suddenly turned dark gray.

Then the heavy rains began to pound on us, even before we could collect our three children and rush to the safety of our room.

Have you ever had this to happen to you? Have your blue skies gone dark without warning? Has life ever caught you in a storm you were not prepared for? Are you there now? Every person is in one of three positions. Either you are in a storm, coming out of a storm, or heading into a storm. What do you do when the storm clouds roll in and life goes from calm to chaos?

I recommend that you do what my family did during that sudden summer shower. Run to safety. Trust Jesus to make the difference. Take refuge in the One who controls the winds and the waves. He makes the difference between chaos and welcome refuge.

Jesus had spent the day teaching and explaining the parables of the kingdom (Mark 4). At the end of this exhausting day, Jesus and His disciples set sail across the Sea of Galilee to retreat from the crowd. With their departure, Mark shifts his focus from the infinite wisdom of Jesus' teachings to the sovereign authority of Jesus' miracles.

In Mark 5, Jesus will cast out a legion of demons, heal an incurable disease, and raise a little girl from the dead. But this series of miracles begins here, when Jesus will calm a raging storm with a simple command. This is the first so-called nature miracle recorded in Mark's gospel. In earlier chapters, Mark reports Jesus exorcising demons and healing diseases. As remarkable as these miracles were, there were many others who claimed the same wonder-working power. But here Mark confronts his readers with the uniqueness of Jesus who demonstrates power over both the wind and the waves.

"WHO IS THIS?"

The story will end with the disciples wondering aloud about the identity of Jesus: "Who then is this, that even the wind and the sea obey him?" (Mark 4:41). This question is the key issue of this miraculous story. What is the true identity of this upstate rabbi from Nazareth? How is it that the wind and waves heed His commands? Who is Jesus?

This miracle provides two answers to this all-important question. First of all, Jesus was truly a human being on earth. He was a man. As they crossed the sea that night, Jesus went to sleep. That's what humans do when they are tired after a long day. Jesus was so exhausted that He slept through the storm. And it seems He would have remained asleep if His disciples had not awakened Him.

We also clearly see in this story that Jesus is the living God. When the disciples awoke Jesus in a panic, the one who lay down like man stood up like God. He rebuked the winds and the waves. And the unruly elements of nature obeyed the voice of Jesus completely and immediately. No wonder the shocked disciples wrestled with the identity of Jesus. Jesus is a human being, like you and me. But He is not just like us. Jesus is the sinless and sovereign Son of the living God.

John declared, "In the beginning was the Word, and the Word was with God, and the Word was God" (John 1:1). Then he said, "And the Word became flesh and dwelt among us" (John 1:14a). Paul said, "He is the image of the invisible God" (Colossians 1:15a). And Paul added, "For in him the whole fullness of deity dwells bodily" (Colossians 2:9). Jesus is God in the flesh. We see this mystery of the incarnation displayed mightily in this story about what Jesus did in a storm.

Before we go any further, the focus of the story must become clear. This story is about Jesus. It is not about the disciples or the storm or even the miracle Jesus performed. It is about Jesus. It is about who He is—His true identity. You will miss the comfort this story provides if you conclude the story is about you, about some personal storm you are going through. The fact that you are in a raging storm is not what matters the most. What matters is whether Jesus is in the boat!

Jesus commanded the disciples to cross over the sea. And the assurance of safe arrival was embedded in the command. Traveling with Jesus, they would not go under. And neither will you! You can trust Jesus in the midst of a storm.

> Thou art the Lord who slept upon the pillow,
> Thou art the Lord who soothed the furious sea,
> What matters the beating wind and tossing billow
> If only we are in the boat with Thee?[1]

Are you in the boat with Jesus? Is Jesus your Savior and Lord? Have you responded to Jesus' call to journey with Him to the other side? If not, run to the cross. If you have, don't run away when trouble comes. Don't be anxious or afraid. You can trust Jesus even when the storm is raging.

JESUS CALLS HIS DISCIPLES INTO A STORM

"On that day, when evening had come, he said to them, 'Let us go across to the other side'" (Mark 4:35). Why did Jesus compel the disciples to cross the sea that evening? The most obvious reason is that Jesus wanted to retreat from the crowd after a long day of ministry. In fact, this is the first of four times Mark's Gospel reports that Jesus fled Galilee to withdraw from the multitudes of people that thronged Him.

Likewise, Jesus led the disciples to travel that evening because He had a ministry appointment on the other side of the sea. When they arrived at the country of the Gerasenes, a deranged man confronted Jesus (more on that encounter in the next chapter). He was possessed by a legion of demons. One reason Jesus would cross the sea this night is to set the demoniac free from the evil spirits that had bound him.

But there is another reason for this evening boat trip. It is the most important reason of all. Jesus planned this trip to lead His disciples into a storm. Did you get that? Jesus led them into a storm with sovereign intentionality. The miraculous quieting of

> **Jesus led the disciples into a storm with sovereign intentionality.**

the storm is the climax of this story. But it is not the point of the story. You will miss the point if you do not come to grips with the truth that the forthcoming storm was a surprise to the disciples but not to Jesus. He knew the howling wind would sweep across the huge lake known as the Sea of Galilee. He knew it because He sent it. And Jesus would lead His disciples to cross the sea to put them on a collision course with a savage windstorm.

Jesus led the disciples to travel across the sea. It was a direct command. "Let us go across to the other side." They had no advance notice they would be traveling. Yet the disciples obeyed. "And leaving the crowd, they took him with them in the boat, just as he was. And other boats were with him" (v. 36). This flotilla casually sailed across the quiet sea for a routine trip. Who knows how many times the disciples had made this trip across the sea? It was as routine as your morning commute. But then the weather suddenly changed without warning.

The Sea of Galilee is a warm, inland body of fresh water that sits 628 feet below sea level, at the bottom of the Jordan Valley. It is surrounded by high mountains. At any point, there can be a severe climate shift, when the cold air descends the mountains to meet the warm surface of the water. The result is near-hurricane-force winds that cause the lazy sea to stir up major waves—up to ten feet high.

This is just what happened that night as Jesus and His disciples crossed the Sea of Galilee: "A great windstorm arose, and the waves were breaking into the boat, so that the boat was already filling" (Mark 4:37). As they traveled along, a whirlwind suddenly erupted. It was like an earthquake hit the sea. And the furious waves viciously attacked their boat. This may have been the worst storm the disciples had ever been in. And as bad as it was for the men to be in those dangerous waters, the waves were rocking the boat, filling it quickly with water. Soon Jesus' disciples were trapped in a flooded boat in the middle of the lake. They could not row to safety. And the winds and waves tossed them about like a rodeo at sea.

It seemed all hope was gone. The disciples, several of whom were experienced fishermen who virtually lived on the sea, concluded that they were going to die in the sea that night.

THOSE UNAVOIDABLE BUT UNEXPECTED STORMS

This crisis moment on the Sea of Galilee confronts us with the fact that the storms of life are inevitable. The sun will not always shine. The sky will not always be blue. The winds will not always be calm. The clouds will not always be pretty. The weather will not always be pleasant. At some point, the placid waters of life will become turbulent.

And the storms of life will come unexpectedly. They happen without warning. You can never put your guard down or your gear up. When things seem to be going well, don't get too comfortable. A storm can come when you least expect it.

It is more than ironic that these experienced fishermen faced a life-threatening storm. The storms of life often overwhelm us in the areas where we seem to be strong. The faithful minister has a dark night of the soul. The godly Christian is attacked by strong temptations. The wise steward faces an unforeseeable financial reversal. Violent storms will come that will overwhelm you. And your skill, strength, experience, resources, and partners will not

> **Faith in the Lord will not prevent storms from coming. And sometimes disobedience to God will lead you into a storm.**

be able to get you through. This, for the record, is how I define a storm in this chapter. It is an overwhelming crisis. If you can easily navigate through it, it is not a real storm. A storm is that desperate situation you would change if you could; but you tried and you can't.

Your faith in the Lord will not prevent storms from coming. Indeed, there are times when disobedience to God will lead you into a storm. Just ask the prophet Jonah. The word of the Lord directed Jonah to go warn the wicked people of Nineveh of impending judgment. But Jonah would rather die than see the Ninevites live. So when the Lord told him to go in one direction to Nineveh, Jonah went in the opposite direction to Tarshish. As a result, the Lord sent a storm to change his mind and turn Jonah in the right direction.

But this was not the situation with the disciples. They were not in a storm because they were in spiritual rebellion. They did exactly what Jesus told them to do. And Jesus was even in the boat with them! Yet their obedience placed them on a collision course with a storm.

It is easy to sit on the banks of the river and pass judgment on others who are going through a storm. But be careful that you are not guilty of spiritual malpractice by misdiagnosing someone else's pain. You don't know what the Lord is doing in someone else's life. For that matter, you do not always know what the Lord is doing in your own situation.

So don't be one of Job's friends. Don't assume that a person who is suffering had to have done something wrong. The fact is there are times Jesus calls His faithful disciples into a storm. But there is good news, as we will soon learn.

JESUS SLEEPS IN THE MIDDLE OF A STORM

What was Jesus doing as the disciples struggled through this storm? "But he was in the stern, asleep on the cushion" (Mark 4:38). What a stark contrast. As the storm raged, Jesus slept. And Mark records a detail omitted by two other Gospel writers.[2] Reflecting the eyewitness account of Peter, Mark says Jesus was "asleep on the cushion." When they set sail, Jesus went to the stern, got comfortable with a pillow, and took a much needed nap. It is the only place in the Gospels that explicitly states Jesus slept.

The fact that Jesus went to sleep that night did not bother the disciples. They knew what kind of day it had been. They knew He was tired. They may have recommended that Jesus get some rest. But they did take issue with the fact that Jesus remained asleep as the situation grew more desperate. Their issue was His seeming indifference. They said, "Teacher, do you not care that we are perishing?" (Mark 4:38b).

Their words are somewhat ironic. Much later, during Jesus' moment of crisis in the garden of Gethsemane, the disciples would fall asleep after Jesus asked them to watch with Him in His agony (Mark 14:32–42). The disciples would sleep when Jesus needed them the most.

JESUS CARES FOR HIS DISCIPLES
IN THE MIDDLE OF A STORM

But Jesus' sleep was not spiritual negligence in a crisis moment. Jesus slept with confidence in God the Father. He practiced the trusting rest of the psalmist: "In peace I will both lie down and sleep; for you alone, O Lord, make me dwell in safety" (Psalm 4:8). Moreover, Jesus' sleep reflected the divine authority He shared with the Father. The Lord of nature does not panic when the winds blow and the waves crash. But the disciples interpreted His sleep another way. They doubted Jesus' steadfast love and sovereign authority. Please don't make their mistakes.

Do not doubt the steadfast love of Jesus in your storm. Note the matter-of-fact way the disciples described their situation: "Teacher, do you not care that we are perishing?" (v. 38b). The disciples were convinced they would die in this storm. Even though Jesus was on board, they only viewed him as a "Teacher," not as the Lord of nature. At least seven of the twelve disciples were fishermen who knew this sea like the back of their hands. Jesus was a carpenter turned rabbi. What did He know about this sea? And what could Jesus do about this storm?

The disciples concluded Jesus could do nothing about the situation. So they did not ask Him to do anything. Instead, they asked whether he cared that they were going to die. Their question was born of fear, desperation, and anger. It was more of a rebuke than a question. They did not think Jesus could stop this storm. But the least He could do would be to pray for them or encourage them . . . or do something. Instead, Jesus was fast asleep on a soft pillow.

And the needy creatures dared to rebuke their sovereign Creator. But they did not challenge the Lord. Their question was simply doubt on display.

It often happens to us as well. We often question the Lord's loving concern when the storm is raging. But let's offer another way to view the matter. An uninvolved Jesus may not demonstrate a lack of concern for your situation. It may be a reflection of His divine refusal to move on your behalf until you get to a place where you recog-

The one who lay down as man stood up as God. Jesus said to the boisterous waves, "Peace! Be still!"

nize that you cannot handle it on your own. The real problem is not divine indifference. It is our belief in human competence. We think we can handle things on our own. Jesus is near. But we let Him sleep, determined to navigate ourselves through the storm. But you cannot believe in Jesus and yourself at the same time. So Jesus continues to wait until you recognize that you cannot make it through the storm without Him. The question is not does Jesus care that you are perishing. It is why have you waited so long to call upon Jesus?

Do not doubt the sovereign authority of Jesus over your storm. Picture this amazing scene. The disciples woke Jesus up. They asked Him if He cared about their impending doom. They did not ask Him to do anything. But Jesus did something that blew their minds. The one who lay down as man stood up as God. Wiping the sleep from His eyes, Jesus stood and surveyed the storm. Then He rebuked the wind, like a father chastising a rebellious child. Then

Jesus said to the boisterous waves, "Peace! Be still!"

For the record, if you stood up in a storm and rebuked the winds and the waves, nothing would happen. But Jesus commanded the storm, "Be quiet! Lay down! And stay that way!" And when Jesus spoke, something happened: "And the wind ceased, and there was a great calm" (Mark 4:39b). At the word of Jesus, the mighty winds immediately ceased to blow. You could say this was nothing but a coincidence. But when the wind ceased there was also a great calm. Typically, when a storm at sea is over, the waves gradually die down. But the authoritative command of Jesus caused the wind to abruptly cease and the waves to immediately die down.

Mark 4–5 record four situations that were beyond control. There was a storm that no one could calm, a demon that no one could tame, a sickness that no one could heal, and a death that no one could avert. But in every situation, Jesus intervened to make the difference. Here Jesus makes the difference in the midst of a storm that no one can navigate.

DO YOU BELIEVE IN MIRACLES?

Do you believe this story? Many people do not. Most unbelievers dismiss the possibility of miracles outright. They believe we live in a closed universe that makes miracles impossible. Others accept the possibility of the supernatural, but would never give Jesus credit for performing such wonders. They embrace the ethical commands of Jesus but reject His supernatural power. Yet many others do not know what to think about the miracles of Jesus.

What about you? How do you read this story? Do you believe Jesus spoke to the elements of nature and they obeyed His voice? You have to pick a side. You cannot kind of believe this story a little bit. The evidence demands a verdict one way or the other. Either you believe Jesus possesses divine, omnipotent, sovereign power or you do not. Where do you stand?

For the sake of argument, let's assume you believe this story. Then let me raise another question. If Jesus can make the winds and waves behave, what situation is there in your life that Jesus cannot handle? It may be a spiritual or physical or relational or financial or emotional storm. It does not matter the category. It does not matter the circumstances. And it does not matter how severe it may be. If Jesus controls the winds and the waves, you can trust Him in your storm. He can say, "Peace! Be still!" to your situation. The stormy waters of your life can become a quiet sea again by the power of Jesus.

JESUS CONFRONTS
HIS DISCIPLES AFTER THE STORM

Mark records three statements Jesus made in this passage. Jesus spoke before the storm arose, prompting the disciples to cross the sea with Him (Mark 4:35). Jesus spoke in the midst of the storm, commanding the violent winds and turbulent waves to cease (Mark 4:39). Then Jesus spoke after the storm calmed, confronting the disciples for their lack of faith (Mark 4:40).

These final statements of Jesus get to the heart of the text. The miracle Jesus performed dramatically answered the question of the disciples. Yes, Jesus cares when it seems the storm is going to take you under. And He is able to bring the tumult to an end. But that is not the point of the story. We know it is not the point because the narrative does not end after the miracle is performed. It does not end with a celebration of the power of Jesus. It ends with a spiritual confrontation. After Jesus rebuked the winds and waves, He rebuked the disciples.

The Lord's rebuke makes it clear that there is divine purpose in and for and beyond your storm. But you most likely will not be able to understand the purpose for the storm until after it is over. Maybe not even then. Ultimately, we see here that the Lord's work in and through your personal storm is for your spiritual development, not your personal well-being. God uses storms to both test us and teach us.

His question was a declaration that they had no right or reason to be afraid . . . that they should have recognized His presence with them in the storm.

Our personal storms test our faith in Jesus. After Jesus calmed the storm, He confronted the disciples with two questions: "Why are you so afraid? Have you still no faith?" (Mark 4:40). These questions called for self-examination. In the midst of the storm, the disciples drew the wrong conclusions about Jesus. Now that the storm was over, Jesus wanted to see if they could draw proper conclusions about Him. What did the disciples think about Jesus after this lifesaving miracle? Jesus tests their faith by confronting their response to the storm.

First, Jesus asked a question about their fear: "Why are you so afraid?" This question states the obvious. The disciples were definitely afraid. But Jesus challenges the reason for their fear. This, too, seems to be obvious. They were afraid because their ship was in the middle of the windswept waters that were overflowing into the ship. At any moment, the violent waves could have capsized the ship and plunged them all to certain death.

Why were they so afraid? It seems the better question would be how could they not be afraid? Yet Jesus rebuked their fears. His question was a declaration that they had no right or reason to be afraid. Jesus was not saying they should have denied the reality of the storm. That was impossible. Jesus was saying that they should have recognized His presence with them in the storm. The storm was powerful. But the power of Jesus is greater. As long as Jesus is with you, what is there to fear?

The Psalms declare the truth about how to deal with our fears. Believe that He is with you:

> Even though I walk through the valley of the shadow of death, I will fear no evil, for you are with me; your rod and your staff, they comfort me. (23:4)

> The Lord is my light and my salvation; whom shall I fear? The Lord is the stronghold of my life; of whom shall I be afraid? (27:1)

> God is our refuge and strength, a very present help in trouble. (46:1)

If the Lord Jesus Christ is with you, you have no reason to be afraid. Take comfort in His presence, even when He seems to be sleeping through your storm.

Then Jesus asked them about their faith: "Have you still no faith?" Jesus questioned their fear because He was with them. But He questioned their faith because of their past experience with Him. Mark 1–3 record multiple miracles Jesus performed over physical sickness and demonic spirits. Jesus even healed Simon Peter's mother-in-law who was bedridden, sick with a fever (1:29–31). The disciples had seen the power of Jesus at work. And they should have trusted Him in the storm. Sure, this is the first nature miracle recorded by Mark. But it is not the first miracle over nature they had witnessed Jesus perform.

JESUS' FIRST MIRACLE

The very first miracle Jesus performed took place at a wedding in Cana of Galilee (John 2:1–11). The newly married couple ran out of wine during the extended wedding feast. It was a crisis that would have embarrassed this family in the community. But Jesus took charge, even though, as He told His mother, "My hour has not yet come" (v. 4). He instructed the servants to pour water into the pots that were used for ritual purification. Then He told them to pour some out and let the governor of the feast taste it. And somewhere between pouring in and pouring out, Jesus worked a miracle.

The master of the feast said it was the best wine that was served. But it was not so good because the grapes were ripe, the fermentation process was excellent, or the wine had proper time to age. It was the best wine because Jesus took control over the natural elements and made them obey His command. This first miracle led the disciples to believe in Jesus (John 2:11). But their faith did not stand when the storm was raging. They did not trust that if Jesus could control the water and make it wine, He can control the waters and make the waves cease.

This is the surprise of faith. Phil Yancey states it this way: "A curious law of reversal seems to be at work in the Gospels: Faith appears where least expected and falters where it should be thriving."[3] Which category do you fall into? It is good and right to trust the Lord in spite of. But it makes no sense to doubt the Lord in spite of. If the Lord has already proven Himself to you, trust Him in the storm. Of course, the circumstances may be different now. But the Lord has not changed. He is still able to do immeasurably beyond all that you can ask or think (Ephesians 3:20).

LEARNING WHO JESUS REALLY IS

The storm also teaches us more about Jesus' identity. Mark describes something as "great" three times in this story. First, a "great" windstorm arose on the Sea of Galilee (Mark 4:37). It was no ordinary storm. It was a super storm. It was a life-threatening storm. Likewise, when Jesus spoke to the winds and the waves, there was "a great calm" (Mark 4:39). The storm did not pass over time. It stopped immediately. The howling winds stopped barking like a chastened puppy. And the storm-tossed waves became still like glass.

Finally, after the miracle, the disciples were "filled with great fear" (Mark 4:41). The disciples were terrified in the storm. But when the storm ceased, their fears did not go away. Their fear transferred from the storm to Jesus and became infinitely greater. It was fear of the sleeping one who woke up to save them from dying in the storm. The MacArthur Study Bible comments: "This was not fear of being harmed by the storm, but a reverence for the supernatural power Jesus had just displayed. The only thing more terrifying than having a storm outside the boat was having God in the boat!"[4]

Peter, Mark's mentor, went through a similar situation on another occasion (see Luke 5:1–11). The crowd pressed Jesus as He stood on the shore. So He got into Peter's boat and sat down to teach, while Peter and his colleagues cleaned their empty nets from a long night of fishing. After teaching the crowds, Jesus commanded Peter to launch into the deep and let down his nets for a catch of fish. Peter objected, "Master, we toiled all night and took nothing! But at your word I will let down the nets" (Luke 5:5).

When Peter did what the Lord commanded, he caught so many fish that his nets began to break. So he called his partners over to help. And when they brought the fish aboard, their ships began to sink. But Peter did not celebrate this unexpected catch. He said to Jesus, "Depart from me, for I am a sinful man, O Lord" (Luke 5:8). Peter recognized that he was an unworthy sinner in the presence of divine authority. So did the disciples. Later, when Jesus stilled the storm, they were again filled with great fear. They were so afraid that they did not dare respond to Jesus' rebuke of their lack of faith. Instead of answering Jesus' questions, they started asking one another a big question. "Who then is this, that even the wind and the sea obey him?" (Mark 4:41)

This is the message of the miracle. This storm experience was meant to teach the disciples more about the true identity of Jesus. Who is this? What manner of man is this? How could this be just a man? They were forced to wrestle with the deity of Jesus because no mere mortal can make the winds and the waves obey him. Only God can do that. The psalmist said, "O Lord God of hosts, who is mighty as you are, O Lord, with your faithfulness all around you? You rule the raging of the sea; when its waves rise, you still them" (Psalm 89:8–9).

When Mark records that Jesus made the winds and waves obey Him, this is not some cute Sunday school story. This is an audacious claim of deity in the person of Jesus. Jesus is Lord over nature. Let the clouds gather. Let the rains fall. Let the winds blow. Let the waves crash. Let the floods rise. When the Lord says, "Peace! Be still!" there will be a great calm. Trust Jesus in your storm.

They came to the other side of the sea, to the country of the Gerasenes. And when Jesus had stepped out of the boat, immediately there met him out of the tombs a man with an unclean spirit. He lived among the tombs. And no one could bind him anymore, not even with a chain, for he had often been bound with shackles and chains, but he wrenched the chains apart, and he broke the shackles in pieces. No one had the strength to subdue him. Night and day among the tombs and on the mountains he was always crying out and cutting himself with stones. And when he saw Jesus from afar, he ran and fell down before him. And crying out with a loud voice, he said, "What have you to do with me, Jesus, Son of the Most High God? I adjure you by God, do not torment me." For he was saying to him, "Come out of the man, you unclean spirit!" And Jesus asked him, "What is your name?" He replied, "My name is Legion, for we are many." And he begged him earnestly not to send them out of the country. Now a great herd of pigs was feeding there on the hillside, and they begged him, saying, "Send us to the pigs; let us enter them." So he gave them permission. And the unclean spirits came out, and entered the pigs, and the herd, numbering about two thousand, rushed down the steep bank into the sea and were drowned in the sea.

The herdsmen fled and told it in the city and in the country. And people came to see what it was that had happened. And they came to Jesus and saw the demon-possessed man, the one who had had the legion, sitting there, clothed and in his right mind, and they were afraid. And those who had seen it described to them what had happened to the demon-possessed man and to the pigs. And they began to beg Jesus to depart from their region. As he was getting into the boat, the man who had been possessed with demons begged him that he might be with him. And he did not permit him but said to him, "Go home to your friends and tell them how much the Lord has done for you, and how he has had mercy on you." And he went away and began to proclaim in the Decapolis how much Jesus had done for him, and everyone marveled.

MARK 5: 1–20

CHAPTER 3

Trusting Jesus
to Set You Free

In Roman Catholicism, St. Jude is the patron saint of lost causes or desperate cases. The name may be more familiar in modern America because of St. Jude's Hospital in Memphis, founded by the entertainer Danny Thomas in 1952 to treat children with catastrophic diseases. Mark 5 is the St. Jude of the New Testament. In this chapter, Mark records three seemingly hopeless cases.

There is a possessed man no one could tame, a sick woman no one could heal, and a dying girl no one could save. These three critical persons were headed to tragic deaths. But Jesus would intervene and save all three.

Mark 5:1–20 records the story of a miraculous exorcism Jesus performed to set a demented man free from spiritual bondage.[1] It is the most definitive statement about demon possession in the Bible.

The Old Testament is clear that the Devil is real. It acknowledges the nature, power, and activity of Satan and his evil forces. Yet it teaches us very little about the work of Satan's demonic forces, much less about demon possession. When Jesus began His public ministry, however, a flurry of satanic activity arose. The Gospels record many confrontations between Jesus and demons. This all-out spiritual warfare continued through the ministry of the apostles.

The New Testament teaches us a great deal about demonic activity. But the story of a particular man is the last word on the subject. (When Jesus asked him "What is your name?" the demon replied, "Legion, for we are many.") Here we find the most extreme case of demon possession in Scripture. The Devil had ravaged this man's life as far as he could, short of death. The man's life was firmly and fully in the Devil's hands. He could not control himself. Society would not and could not help him. "Legion" was on a collision course with a tragic death. But Jesus intervened. Jesus set him free. Jesus made him different.

> The power of Jesus has not changed. The one who delivered Legion is alive and well.

The point of this chapter is that the power of Jesus has not changed. Your circumstances are not as extreme as Legion's, even though it may feel that way. But don't focus on Legion. Focus on the Lord. The power of Jesus has not changed. The one who delivered Legion, a man controlled by many demons, is alive and well. Jesus has the power to set you free from any evil thing that has you bound.

Young people say, "It's all good!" That's cool slang but bad theology. All is not good. All is not inherently good. All is not individually good. All is not immediately good. We live in a world that is sin-scarred, self-centered, and Satan-dominated. There are many things that happen in this world that are as far from good as up is from down, night is from day, black is from white. It is not all good. In fact, there are many things that are evil.

"Evil" may sound like an old-fashioned word in our society. The modern mind claims there is no such thing, never was. And we grope about for explanations when bad things happen in the world. How about this explanation? It is evil. Just look around our world. Just watch the news—local or international. Just stare into the mirror.

The prophet Jeremiah said, "The heart is deceitful above all things, and desperately sick; who can understand it?" (Jeremiah 17:9). We have deep-seated evil within us that we cannot even understand, much less change on our own. Again, Jeremiah asked,

Where do you stand in this battle against evil . . . the evil in the world within you?

"Can the Ethiopian change his skin or the leopard his spots? Then also you can do good who are accustomed to do evil" (Jeremiah 13:23). We have as much hope of doing true good as a leopard has of changing his spots. Instead, we are bound by evil that we cannot control. It makes us desire things we should not desire. It makes us choose things we should not choose. It makes us say things we should not say. It makes us do things we should not do. It makes us go places we should not go.

Our culture is quick to assert one's right to live as one chooses. But it does not tell us every choice has consequences. In fact, the consequences of some choices will limit future choices. Sure, we are free moral agents who have the right to choose for ourselves between good and evil. But certain choices—evil choices—will enslave us. And evil creates bondage seductively. There you are, celebrating your freedom to do what you want to do. And you cannot recognize that you are bound to your evil desires—until you try to stop doing what you desire. Ultimately, that's what hell is all about. Hell is where the evil person will do what he wants to do without God for all eternity.

Where do you stand in this battle against evil? I am not talking about the evil in the world around you. I am talking about the evil in the world within you. Are you winning that battle? Does evil have you bound? Have you said yes to something that you now cannot say no to? Are you struggling with a habit? Do you want true and lasting victory over the besetting sins that wage war against your soul?

I have good news for you. Jesus can set you free. Jesus can give you a fresh start, another chance, and a new beginning. Jesus can make the difference in your life. What Jesus did for Legion He can do for you. In Mark 5:1–20, we see the power of Jesus over evil put on display in three dramatic encounters.

JESUS ENCOUNTERS A DEMENTED MAN

"They came to the other side of the sea, to the country of the Gerasenes" (Mark 5:1). Bible scholars are not sure exactly where the country of the Gerasenes is. But the real issue here is not about where Jesus and His disciples landed. The point is that they landed. To flee the crowds, Jesus led the disciples to cross the Sea of Galilee (Mark 4:35–41). On their way to the other side, Jesus and the disciples were engulfed in a violent storm on the sea. The disciples thought they would die in the storm that night. But Jesus intervened to demonstrate His power over the violent winds and waves—the natural elements. Now, in a dramatic encounter with a man known as Legion, Jesus displays His power over the supernatural elements in the invisible realm.

Jesus had conquered a storm at sea. Now He will face a tempest in a man's life. This is another reason why you can trust Him in every situation. Jesus controls not just the external, outward elements of your daily life. Jesus can control the internal forces in your life. Let Jesus be Lord over both your external problems and your internal pain. Jesus can handle whatever happens *to* you. And Jesus can handle whatever is happening *in* you.

The Bible is filled with stories of suffering. In Scripture, we meet wicked people who suffer for their sins. And we meet even more righteous people who suffer because of their obedience to God. You cannot read the Bible objectively without concluding that suffering is an inevitable part of life and faith. In a real sense, Scripture is about suffering. But no person in Scripture suffered more than the demented man in our text.

Job is considered the greatest example of suffering in the Bible. "The suffering of Job" has become a cliché. But not even Job suffered more than Legion. Mark describes a troubled man in a pitiful condition (Mark 5:3-5), marked by antisocial behavior and inner turmoil, coupled with superhuman strength and constant torment.

His antisocial behavior: "And when Jesus had stepped out of the boat, immediately there met him out of the tombs a man with an unclean spirit" (v. 2). Then Mark repeats: "He lived among the tombs" (v. 3). And he will later say it again: "Night and day among the tombs and on the mountains he was always crying out and cutting himself with stones" (v. 5).

Inner turmoil. His inner turmoil drove this man away from his family and friends. He was no longer welcome in the community. People did not want to be anywhere near him. And, frankly, he did not want to be anywhere near them. He could not live with the living. So he moved in with the dead. He lived among the tombs. These tombs were not in some carefully manicured cemetery. This was definitely no place you would plant flowers and sit to remember the dearly departed. These tombs were caves cut into the hillside where the living placed the dead. Sane and normal people would not go anywhere near these tombs. But they were haunts and hangouts for unclean spirits. This is where this demented man lived. He made his dwelling among the tombs. The living dead resided among the buried dead.

Superhuman strength. The community dealt with this demented man the only way they knew how. They bound him in chains. This may sound primitive. But don't be too quick to judge. We are not that far removed from the days of straitjackets and padded cells. Things have changed, but not for the better. We now prescribe mind-numbing drugs to troubled people. These medications may calm erratic behavior. But they cannot address internal problems. In regard to helping people change, we do no better than the ancients did.

His supernatural strength evoked fear and turned Legion into a monster. The people of the community chained this man to keep him from doing any harm to them. But the demonic forces within caused him to grow in strength: "And no one could bind him anymore, not even with a chain, for he had often been bound with shackles and chains, but he wrenched the chains apart, and he broke the shackles in pieces. No one had the strength to subdue him" (Mark 5:3b–4).

There was a time when chains worked to deal with Legion. But not anymore. Over time, he grew stronger until his power became superhuman. Supernatural. He would effortlessly rip off the shackles from his feet and the chains from his hands. No one could subdue him. The Greek word "subdue" in verse 4 means to tame a wild animal. Incidentally, it is the same word used in James 3:8 when the apostle warns that "no human being can tame the tongue."

The use of the word "subdue" in this story indicates the severity of this man's condition. Think about it. You tame wild animals, not human beings. But demons had so thoroughly changed his personality that he had become virtually a wild man. "Legion is Samson gone berserk."[2]

Constant torment. This demented man was strong enough to break the chains and shackles that bound him. But he was not strong enough to expel the demons that tormented him: "Night and day among the tombs and on the mountains he was always crying out and cutting himself with stones" (Mark 5:5). Legion suffered ongoing agony that tormented him morning, noon, and night. He was a restless soul. He would disappear into the tombs. Then he would dart up to the mountaintops. Back and forth he went, day after day. But people always knew where Legion was, because they could hear him crying out with unearthly shrieks and obscene screams. His torment led to self-destructive behavior. He would cut himself with stones, as if he were trying to rip the unclean spirit from his flesh.

This is a dramatic picture of the power of evil in a human life. I doubt you will find another case of demon possession this extreme. But the underlying reality of turmoil is at work in every person who does not know Jesus Christ. The much admired Oxford scholar C. S. Lewis described his life before conversion as "a zoo of lusts, a bedlam of ambitions, a nursery of fears, a harem of fondled hatreds. My name was Legion."[3] This is the story of every unsaved person. Every unbeliever is a victim of spiritual bondage. Paul describes life without spiritual deliverance this way: "And you were dead in the trespasses and sins in which you once walked, following the course of this world, following the prince of the power of the air, the spirit that is now at work in the sons of disobedience—among whom we all once lived in the passions of our flesh, carrying out the desires of the body and the mind, and were by nature children of wrath, like the rest of mankind" (Ephesians 2:1–3).

Note that Paul wrote these words to those who believed in Jesus. They were saved, but they needed to remember what Christ saved them from so that they would not fall into bondage. Even Christians can fall into bondage to sin. The warning of the story of Legion is that the power of evil is a force that is not to be played with. You can become caught up in something you cannot get yourself out of. But Jude announced, "[He] is able to keep you from stumbling and to present you blameless before the presence of his glory with great joy" (Jude 24).

We see a powerful illustration of the difference Jesus makes in His encounter with a spiritual army (Mark 5:6–13).

JESUS ENCOUNTERS A SPIRITUAL ARMY

Legion did not act the way he did on his own. It is not right to simply write him off as a crazy man. He was not schizophrenic. His problem was not psychological. His was a spiritual issue; he was possessed by many demons. Satanic angels had kidnapped his personality and worked evil through him. He truly could not control himself. Society could not do anything to stop or help or change him. He was bound by these demonic forces, and nothing could set him free.

That is, until he met Jesus. The power of demons was no match for the power of Jesus.

The demons bow to Jesus: "And when he saw Jesus from afar, he ran and fell down before him" (v. 6). The satanic powers that bound this man were evil, destructive, and uncontrollable. But when this troubled man entered the presence of the Lord Jesus, the demonic forces within him bowed in submission to the authority of Jesus. "Crying out with a loud voice, he said, 'What have you to do with me, Jesus, Son of the Most High God?'" (Mark 5:7).

On one occasion, Jesus delivered a demon-possessed man who was mute. When Jesus set him free, the mute man spoke and "the crowds marveled, saying, 'Never was anything like this seen in Israel'" (Matthew 9:33). The Pharisees disagreed. "He casts out demons by the prince of demons," they rebutted (Matthew 9:34). But the demons within Legion make a clear distinction: "What have you to do with me . . . ?" (Mark 5:7). The unclean spirit in this man made it clear that Jesus is not one of them. Jesus has a divine nature, sovereign authority, and holy purpose. He is not a man with an unclean spirit. The demons knew his true identity: "Jesus, Son of the Most High God" (v. 7).

> **Now the demons recognize Jesus as the "Son of the Most High God," not merely human but truly divine.**

Earlier, the winds and the waves had obeyed Jesus' voice, and the churning seas had become "a great calm" (Mark 4:39). The disciples responded by asking one another: "Who then is this, that even the wind and the sea obey him?" (v. 41). So Mark 4 ends with the disciples' question unanswered. But they got their answer several hours later. As they stood on the shore of the country of the Gerasenes, a wild man filled with demons announced before them that Jesus is the Son of the Most High God.

It seems these demons had good theology. They recognized the dual nature of Christ. They knew Jesus was the God-Man. The name "Jesus" affirms the humanity of Christ. He was one of us. Jesus was a man. But He was infinitely more than Mary's baby. This human being was divine. The demons declare Jesus is "the Son of the Most High God." This title is a statement about both God the Father and God the Son.

The Father is "the Most High God." This was a divine title used by both Jews and Gentiles to identify the one true and living God of Israel and to distinguish Him from all false idol gods. And now the demons recognize Jesus as the "Son of the Most High God." They recognize that Jesus is not merely human but truly divine. He is God in the flesh.

The demons recognize the deity, authority, and sovereignty of Jesus. Yet they dare to issue Him a command. Speaking as one, they say, "I adjure you by God, do not torment me" (Mark 5:7). The word "adjure" means to cause one to make an oath. These demons seek to get Jesus to swear in the name of God that He will not torment them. They demand a truce that will protect them from the power and authority of Jesus. This desperate request is a glimpse at how sinister evil is. The very demons who tormented this man for God knows how long, now beg Jesus not to torment them. Satan and his evil forces are truly the greatest hypocrites of all.

Why did these demons fear Jesus? Matthew and Luke's accounts shed light. Matthew reports the demons asked Jesus, "Have you come here to torment us before the time?" (Matthew 8:29b). Not only do demons have good Christology, they also have good eschatology. They know who Jesus is. And they know what the end is going to be. The demons knew they would face a day of reckoning. But they thought Jesus was not going according to schedule. They were afraid that Jesus had come to execute final judgment early.

Luke adds, "And they begged him not to command them to depart into the abyss" (Luke 8:31). The abyss is the place of the dead. It is the true home of demonic spirits. And it is a place of torment for unclean spirits. The demons would prefer the comfort of a ravaged soul than the torment of the abyss. It is the last place they want to go, which gives us a little hint of what hell must be like, doesn't it?

JESUS DISPLAYS AUTHORITY
OVER SATAN AND HIS DEMONS

There was a reason why these demons were going to such desperate measures to get Jesus to leave them alone: For He was saying to him, "Come out of the man, you unclean spirit!" (Mark 5:8).

See the power of Jesus on display! Jesus did not perform exorcisms by formula, ritual, or incantation. With divine authority, He simply commanded the demons to leave the man.

At some point in this encounter, Jesus asked, "What is your name?" (Mark 5:9). We do not know who this question was directed to, the man or the demon. Both answered, "My name is Legion, for we are many."

Legion is one of two persons in the New Testament who were possessed by multiple demons. The other is Mary Magdalene, from whom Jesus cast out seven demons (Mark 16:9). In addition, Jesus told a parable about an unclean spirit who recruits seven demons worse than himself to help him repossess a man's heart (Matthew 12:43–45).

In the case of Legion, an army of demons possessed him! A legion was the largest Roman military unit. It consisted of six thousand soldiers at full strength. No wonder no one could bind this man! There may have been more demons in this man than were people in this community. One man outnumbered them. This was an extreme case of demon possession that we cannot imagine. But when this army of demons met Jesus, they had no choice but to bow to His authority.

The man known as Legion begged Jesus "earnestly not to send them out of the country." Instead, seeing a large herd of pigs feeding on a nearby hillside, he "begged him, saying, 'Send us to the pigs; let us enter them'" (Mark 5:10, 12). In these verses, the demons begged Jesus twice. First, they begged Jesus not to send them out of coun-

> **Notice, the demons could not remain in that person or that place without the approval of Jesus.**

try. This passage is not grounds for teaching that there are territorial spirits that work in special locations. We should just take the text at face value. For whatever reason, these demons did not want to be expelled from this region. So they begged Jesus to be sent to enter the nearby herd of pigs.

The fact that these demons beg Jesus makes it clear that the power of Satan is limited. Satan's power is real and great and more than we can handle as mere humans. But Satan is not omnipotent. This is why the demons conceded the fact that they could not remain in the man once Jesus commanded them to go. They did not put up a fight. But they pleaded not to be deported from the country and banished to the abyss (v. 10; Luke 8:31). Notice, the demons could not remain in that person or that place without the approval of Jesus.

Satan cannot move without divine permission. Before every move Satan made in Job's life, he had to seek divine permission. Jesus told Peter that Satan had been asking to sift him as wheat (Luke 22:31–32). But note that he had to ask! So it is in every situation. Sure, the Devil is busy. But he is busy doing only what the sovereign Lord allows him to do. The Devil is God's devil. Satan is "God's lapdog." He cannot move without divine permission. We have an affirmation of this fact when the demons that had terrorized Legion begged Jesus just to stay in the area.

Likewise, we see here that the power of Satan is destructive. The demons beg Jesus not to expel them from that country. Then they beg Jesus to send them into a nearby herd of pigs. They have to destroy something. If it can no longer be this man, it might as well be a group of pigs. "So he gave them permission. And the unclean spirits came out, and entered the pigs, and the herd, numbering about two thousand, rushed down the steep bank into the sea and were drowned in the sea" (Mark 5:13).

This is the most controversial verse of the story. People read this verse and accuse Jesus of doing something unethical by permitting the demons to destroy these pigs. They allege Jesus is encouraging the mistreatment of animals. Yes, the destruction of the pigs would have an adverse effect on the local economy. But no apologies are needed here. The soul of this man was worth infinitely more than the herd of pigs.

Jesus permitted the demons to destroy these pigs to give clear evidence that the demon-possessed man had been set free. Even the onlookers knew that the evil forces that had this man bound had been sovereignly dismissed. That is the point of the story. Jesus can set you free from any evil thing that has you bound. It may be a sin of the flesh. Or it may be a sin of the spirit. But Jesus can set you free. Paul says, "He has delivered us from the domain of darkness and transferred us to the kingdom of his beloved Son, in whom we have redemption, the forgiveness of sins" (Colossians 1:13-14).

JESUS ENCOUNTERS A FRIGHTENED CROWD

You would think this story could not get any more dramatic than the encounter Jesus has with the demented man who was possessed by an army of demons. But the most dramatic part of the story takes place after the miraculous exorcism. The closing section of this narrative teaches us important lessons about human depravity and Christian discipleship.

A lesson about human depravity. The news of this miraculous exorcism traveled fast: "The herdsmen fled and told it in the city and in the country. And people came to see what it was that had happened" (Mark 5:14). When the people of the community came to Jesus, they were stunned by what they saw and heard.

The people saw an incredible sight. The demon-possessed man who had terrorized the community was now a changed man: "They . . . saw the demon-possessed man, the one who had had the legion, sitting there, clothed and in his right mind" (v. 15). What a change! The man was no longer frantically racing about from the mountains to the tombs. He was now sitting at the feet of Jesus. His demon possession may have led to sexual perversion, as he had run about naked. But now he was fully clothed. He had been a demented man characterized by antisocial behavior, superhuman strength, and constant torment. But now he was in his right mind. He was no longer what he used to be. He was a new person. Jesus made the difference!

How do you think the people responded when they met this "new" man? Mark reports, "They were afraid" (Mark 5:15b). This is ironic. We are never told the people were afraid of this demon-possessed man. They may have even become used to his antics. But they were afraid of the one who cast the demons out of him. Bible commentator Lawrence Richards wrote: "How strange! Human beings often fear the power of God that is able to deliver, but not the power of the evil that enslaves us."[4] What are you afraid of?

Then the people heard an incredible story: "And those who had seen it described to them what had happened to the demon-possessed man and to the pigs" (Mark 5:16). The herdsmen did not want to be held responsible for the loss of the pigs. So when the city came out to them, they retold what happened with Legion and the pigs. But in their efforts to avoid culpability, they gave a clear and compelling testimony to the power of Jesus. The Lord will never be without a witness! And He can raise up a testimony to His greatness in some strange places.

"And they began to beg Jesus to depart from their region" (Mark 5:17) When I was a boy preacher, I preached a sermon on Mark 5:17. I called it, "The Day Man Prayed for Jesus to Leave." It was not a detailed exposition of the story. It was a sermon based on a young preacher's devotional observation. And the thing that jumped out to me was the fact they begged Jesus to leave. You would think they would have said, "Jesus, please stay here! We have more crazy people around here for you to change." After seeing the difference Jesus makes, you would think they would have elected Jesus to some high office to lead the region. But they instead begged Jesus to leave!

Here is a lesson in human depravity. Having seen the power of Jesus at work, these people still did not believe. They were so consumed with their way of life that they had no regard for the rescue of a human life or the presence of the Lord of life. This reality slaps us in the face with the fact that miracles don't save lost people. The unbelieving heart can see the greatest of miracles and remain in unbelief. Only God can change hard hearts.

A lesson about Christian discipleship. Jesus is a gentleman. He does not stay where He is not wanted. So when the citizens deported Him from the region, Jesus complied. Jesus and the disciples walked to the shore to get back into their boats.

"As he was getting into the boat, the man who had been possessed with demons begged him that he might be with him" (Mark 5:18). A would-be, thirteenth disciple tried to get on the boat, "the man who had been possessed with demons." Isn't that wonderful? When Jesus sets you free, you are no longer what you used to be. Paul says, "Therefore, if anyone is in Christ, he is a new creation. The old has passed away; behold, the new has come" (2 Corinthians 5:17).

This new man begged to be with Jesus. It is the third time someone begged Jesus in this story. The demons begged Jesus not to send them out of the country but into a nearby herd of pigs (Mark 5:10, 12). And the people begged Jesus to leave their country (Mark 5:17). Then the delivered man begged Jesus to go with Him (Mark 5:18). Sitting at the feet of Jesus, he adopted the posture of a disciple. Now he pleaded to enter the life of a disciple: "that he might be with him." Discipleship is to follow Jesus that you may be with Him and thus become like Him.

> **Jesus denied this man's request because He had a greater assignment for him: to tell his people how much the Lord had done for him.**

Mark reports that Jesus "did not permit him but said to him, 'Go home to your friends and tell them how much the Lord has done for you, and how he has had mercy on you.'" (Mark 5:19).

This man's request is the most reasonable request made of Jesus in this story. Yet it is the only request Jesus denied. Jesus granted the demons' request to enter the herd of swine. And Jesus granted the citizens' request that He leave their region. But when this delivered man begged to go with Him, Jesus said no. It was a good and godly request. But Jesus refused. He denied this man's personal request because He had a greater assignment for him. Jesus commanded him to go home to his people and tell them how much the Lord had done for him.

Note that Jesus did not instruct him to tell *what* the Lord had done, but *how much* the Lord had mercifully done for him. "And he went away and began to proclaim in the Decapolis how much Jesus had done for him, and everyone marveled" (Mark 5:20).

Jesus had ordered this man to go tell "how much the Lord has done for you" (v. 19). But the man went and proclaimed how much *Jesus* had done for him. Jesus told him to give the credit to God the Father. But he gave the credit to Jesus. Yet he did not fail to give credit where credit was due. By proclaiming Jesus he glorified the Father. Jesus declared, "I and the Father are one" (John 10:30).

Jesus' commission to Legion is a standing order for every person who has experienced the sparing mercy of God. It would be wonderful to be with Jesus. But He has left us here for a reason. Why do you think Jesus has left you here? We have work to do. We have a calling to accomplish. We have a mission to fulfill. It is a simple assignment. We are to tell our family and friends how much the Lord has done for us and how He has shown mercy to us. We should tell everyone we can about the difference Jesus makes.

And when Jesus had crossed again in the boat to the other side, a great crowd gathered about him, and he was beside the sea. Then came one of the rulers of the synagogue, Jairus by name, and seeing him, he fell at his feet and implored him earnestly, saying, "My little daughter is at the point of death. Come and lay your hands on her, so that she may be made well and live." And he went with him. And a great crowd followed him and thronged about him.

While he was still speaking, there came from the ruler's house some who said, "Your daughter is dead. Why trouble the Teacher any further?" But overhearing what they said, Jesus said to the ruler of the synagogue, "Do not fear, only believe." And he allowed no one to follow him except Peter and James and John the brother of James. They came to the house of the ruler of the synagogue, and Jesus saw a commotion, people weeping and wailing loudly. And when he had entered, he said to them, "Why are you making a commotion and weeping? The child is not dead but sleeping." And they laughed at him. But he put them all outside and took the child's father and mother and those who were with him and went in where the child was. Taking her by the hand he said to her, "Talitha cumi," which means, "Little girl, I say to you, arise." And immediately the girl got up and began walking (for she was twelve years of age), and they were immediately overcome with amazement. And he strictly charged them that no one should know this, and told them to give her something to eat.

MARK 5:21–24, 35–43

CHAPTER 4

Trusting Jesus
at a Dead End

There was a time when Jairus would have never been caught in a crowd like this. As one of the rulers of the local synagogue, he had seen his share of upstart rabbis, self-proclaimed healers, and wannabe messiahs. It all made Jairus cynical, appropriately so. When Jairus first heard the reports about Jesus of Nazareth, I imagine he instinctively said to himself, "Here we go again."

But that was then. This is now. His desperate circumstances now collided with his conservative theology. Life happened to Jairus. There was a crisis at his house. It was a parent's worst nightmare. His twelve-year-old daughter was at the point of death. She was his only daughter (Luke 8:42). We do not know any of the details of her sickness. But whatever it was that afflicted her was life threatening.

Jairus and his wife did all they could to find a cure for their beloved daughter. They offered fervent prayers, spent a small fortune, and called in every favor possible. Nothing worked. At some point, the doctors did all they could for her. She was finally sent home to die. Family and friends maintained a vigil there, hoping for the best but expecting the worst.

The crisis at Jairus's house is a stark reminder of the universal nature of trouble, sickness, and death. No one is exempt. Trouble confronts the rich and the poor. Sickness attacks the godly and the ungodly. Death takes the young and the old. There is a technical, theological term for this reality: life. Think about it. Jairus had wealth, status, and influence. As the ruler of the synagogue he was a devout man. But these factors could not stop his daughter from getting sick. And none of them could heal her. This is the universal fact of life. Whoever you are, trouble knows your address. And it will show up at your house sooner or later.

THE RIGHT RESPONSE: COME TO JESUS

This story of Jairus's daughter also teaches us of the proper response to life's desperate circumstances. Jairus took his problem to Jesus. He came to Jesus because a need drove him there. This is often the case. I can testify that this is how I came to Jesus. What about you? Few people find Jesus at the end of a search for truth. Most people come to Jesus in the midst of an overwhelming problem.

We do not come because we want to do something for Jesus. We come because we need Jesus to do something for us. This is how Jairus came to Jesus that day, with an overwhelming need. But Jesus did not turn him away. He agreed to go home with Jairus to heal his daughter (Mark 5:24).

The miracle at Jairus's house is the climax of a series of miracles that demonstrates the supernatural power and sovereign authority of Jesus (Mark 4–5). We have seen that Jesus is Lord over the elements of nature and the world of demons. In the middle of helping Jairus, Jesus would quickly display His power over the threat of sickness, as a woman simply touched His garment (Mark 5:25–34; see next chapter for the in-depth account). Now we will see that Jesus is Lord over the finality of death.

Death does not have the last word in life. Jesus has the last word in every situation—including death, of which He partook and conquered. As the writer of Hebrews declares, "Since therefore the children share in flesh and blood, he himself likewise partook of the same things, that through death he might destroy the one who has the power of death, that is, the devil, and deliver all those who through fear of death were subject to lifelong slavery" (Hebrews 2:14–15).

JESUS' FINAL WORD
WHEN DISAPPOINTMENT SPEAKS

After departing the country of the Gerasenes and heading back across the Sea of Galilee, Jesus landed near Capernaum. There a large crowd awaited Him. In this crowd was Jairus, a ruler of the synagogue, one of the lay elders who oversaw the work and worship of the assembly.

The presence of Jairus may have surprised many in the crowd. The representatives of the religious establishment typically rejected Jesus, with rare exceptions. Perhaps Jairus himself had previously warned the members of his synagogue about so-called miracle workers like Jesus. But there he was among the crowd that day. A desperate need drove him to Jesus.

Before Jairus was a spiritual and social leader, the entire community knew about his family situation. And so their hearts went out to him. When Jairus showed up to meet Jesus, people made room for him to get to the front of the crowd.

As Jesus disembarked, Jairus was one of the first to meet Him. But he did not introduce himself as the ruler of the synagogue. Titles, position, and status don't matter when your children are in trouble. Jairus did not kiss Jesus' cheek, which would have been a typical greeting. He fell at Jesus' feet with humility, dependence, and submission.

"My little daughter is at the point of death," Jairus implored (Mark 5:23). This "little daughter" was twelve years old (v. 42). In that society, she was on the verge of womanhood. It would not be long before she would be married with children. Yet Jairus called her his "little daughter." It did not matter if she was twelve, twenty-one, or fifty. She would always be his little girl.

And she was at the point of death. No cure for her disease was found. Jairus and his wife had exhausted all options to cure their daughter of whatever sickness afflicted her. Her severe condition had grown rapidly worse. She could succumb at any moment. In fact, by going to Jesus for help, Jairus would risk never seeing his daughter alive again. But while there was any sliver of hope, he could not just sit there and watch her die. He had to do something. Anything. So he came and pleaded with Jesus to heal his daughter.

Jairus pleaded, "Come and lay your hands on her, so that she may be made well and live" (Mark 5:23).

Jesus consented to help: "And he went with him" (Mark 5:24). This statement is a picture of the compassion of Jesus. You do know that He could have healed the girl from right where He stood, don't you? On another occasion, when Jesus agreed to heal a centurion's servant, messengers stopped Him in His tracks before He made it to the house (Luke 7:1–10). The centurion said that he was not worthy to have Jesus come under his roof (see vv. 6–7). But he believed that Jesus could heal his servant by simply speaking the word of command. Jesus marveled at his faith and healed the servant without going to the centurion's house. Yet Jesus chose to go to Jairus's house. It was an act of compassionate love. And the Lord is gracious enough to show up where you need Him the most.

JAIRUS'S UNEXPECTED INTERRUPTION

As Jairus led the way through the crowd, Jesus felt something. He stopped and began to look around. A woman had touched his garments (Mark 5:25–27). "Who touched my garments?" Jesus asked (v. 30). In the next chapter we will look at the reasons an omniscient God asked this question. But one reason Jesus had the woman identify herself as the one was for Jairus's benefit. I am sure Jairus did not feel that way as it was happening. It was just the opposite. Jairus may have been happy for the woman's healing.

But he no doubt felt it was an interruption that delayed Jesus from getting to his daughter who was at the point of death. This woman had been sick of a blood disorder for twelve years (v. 25). But Jairus's daughter could die at any moment. Why was Jesus wasting time?

The reason was simple. Jesus took His time to talk to the woman because He knew what was coming—Jairus's daughter *would* revive. And Jesus stopped to get the woman's confession to build up Jairus's faith in advance of tragic news he would soon receive.

BAD NEWS FROM HOME

Once the woman had been healed, her confession received, and her faith commended, Jairus was ready to lead Jesus to his house. As they were about to resume the walk, things went from bad to worse.

Don't miss that. The presence of Jesus did not automatically make things better. Jairus was ready to once more resume the journey with Jesus. Yet the situation deteriorated: "While he was still speaking, there came from the ruler's house some who said, 'Your daughter is dead'" (Mark 5:35).

With Jesus there is always hope. Nothing is too hard for Him.

Jairus received the heartbreaking news: "Your daughter is dead. Why trouble the Teacher any further?" This rhetorical question made two statements. First, this question said it was no longer necessary for Jairus to worry Jesus about going to his house anymore. At this point, Jairus could just let Jesus go about His business. There may have been many others Jesus could help. But there was nothing else that could be done for Jairus's daughter. So don't trouble Jesus further. The second was, all hope is gone. Jesus can't do anything to change the matter.

The messengers were wrong on both points. First of all, you never trouble Jesus when you bring Him your troubles. Jesus is not like some people who ask how you are doing and then hope you won't really tell them. Jesus is a friend to the disappointed. He cares about your situation. And He calls, "Come to me, all who labor and are heavy laden, and I will give you rest" (Matthew 11:28).

Likewise, with Jesus there is always hope. Nothing is too hard for Him. The Lord is never too late. David testified, "You have turned for me my mourning into dancing; you have loosed my sackcloth and clothed me with gladness" (Psalm 30:11). When things go from bad to worse, Jesus is there to comfort, strengthen, and intervene.

JESUS' TWO COMMANDS TO JAIRUS

Jesus was there for Jairus when disappointment spoke: "But overhearing what they said, Jesus said to the ruler of the synagogue, 'Do not fear, only believe'" (Mark 5:36). Jesus did not allow the bearers of bad news to have the last word. Having heard the report of the messengers, Jesus gave Jairus two commands.

First, Jesus commanded Jairus not to be afraid. When Jairus heard that his daughter was dead, fear gripped him before grief could reach him. The news had sent Jairus into shock. He was more afraid than he was sorrowful. But Jesus told him to shake it off. In the original Greek, the imperative "Do not fear" has a grammatical emphasis that forbids the continuation of something that is already taking place. Fear had already consumed Jairus's heart and mind. Jesus said to him, in effect, "Stop it! Stop being afraid."

Likewise, Jesus commanded Jairus to keep believing. The command to "only believe" was a call to a present and continual faith. Jesus told Jairus to stop being afraid but don't stop believing. He had enough faith to leave his dying daughter at home to come to Jesus and ask for His healing help. But disappointing news replaced his faith with fear. But Jesus commanded him to keep believing. And note that Jesus did not tell Jairus what was going to happen next. He did not announce, "I am going to raise your daughter from the dead." He let Jairus remain in the darkness of disappointment. But in the darkness, He commanded Jairus not to let go of His hand.

"Only believe."

This is the word of Jesus to you today. Life is filled with disappointments. Promises are not kept. Dreams are unfulfilled. Goals are not reached. Hopes are not materialized. People are not what they seem to be. And in the valley of disappointment, you are tempted to give up or give in or give out. But don't let your disappointments have the last word. Do not fear. Only believe. Harry Ironside wrote, "When we are at the end of all natural resources the same blessed words come home to our hearts to give peace and confidence today."[1] Whatever disappointment you face, Jesus says to stop being afraid and keep believing.

Keep believing when sickness comes.

Keep believing when you lose your job.

Keep believing when family problems arise.

Keep believing when help is delayed.

Keep believing when you feel like giving up.

Keep believing when death stares you in the face.

Keep believing when all hope is gone.

JAIRUS'S RESPONSE

The messengers from Jairus's house brought the sad news that his daughter had died. It was all over, as far as they were concerned. There was no reason for Jesus to go to Jairus's house. All hope was gone. But Jesus challenged Jairus not to fear but to keep believing. These radical commands left Jairus with a decision to make. He could accept the report of the messengers. Or he could heed the commands of Jesus. It is the choice we all have to make at some time or another. Will you believe what the circumstances say? Or will you believe what Jesus says?

Jairus chose to believe the word of the Lord. And they pressed their way to Jairus's house.

"And he allowed no one to follow him except Peter and James and John the brother of James" (Mark 5:37). This is the first of several times Jesus permits this inner circle of His disciples to be exclusive witnesses of an important moment in His ministry. Only Peter, James, and John witnessed the transfiguration of Jesus, when His divine glory shone through His human flesh (Mark 9:2). And only these three were with Jesus in His moments of agony, as He prayed to the Father in the garden of Gethsemane (Mark 14:33).

Jesus, Jairus, and the inner circle finally made it to the house: "They came to the house of the ruler of the synagogue, and Jesus saw a commotion, people weeping and wailing loudly" (Mark 5:38). Bad news travels fast, doesn't it?

By the time Jairus made it home, friends and family had already gathered. And the professional mourners were there. In the ancient Near East, the dead were buried immediately. Families paid their respects to the dead by open displays of mourning. They would hire flute players to play loudly, almost encouraging loud mourning. And they would also hire a wailing woman to lead the mourning. In fact, the wealthier the family, the more professional mourners they hired to grieve the dead. With Jairus being a ruler of the synagogue, many people gathered at the house to honor him by grieving with the family over the death of his daughter. So when Jesus arrived at the house, there was a great commotion. People were weeping and wailing loudly.

DEAD . . . OR ALIVE?

"And when he had entered, he said to them, 'Why are you making a commotion and weeping?'" (Mark 5:39a). This is a strange question. Weeping and wailing are natural responses to death. To ask a grieving person why they are weeping is incredibly insensitive. What else are you supposed to do when a loved one dies? But Jesus deemed the commotion to be out of place. Overmuch sorrow is inappropriate when the Lord of life is present.

Jesus questioned the place of the loud commotion by saying, "The child is not dead but sleeping" (Mark 5:39b). This is the most difficult statement of the text. What did Jesus mean when He said the girl was not dead but sleeping? Some Bible commentators read this statement literally to mean that the girl was in a deep, sleep-like coma. And those who have a hard time believing that Jesus raised the dead rush to adopt this position. It makes it easier for them to deal with this story. But it does not help anyone escape the confrontation about the identity of Jesus in this story. If Jesus is only a mere man, it is no easier for Him to call someone from a coma than to raise someone from the dead. Either Jesus is Lord over life and death or He is not.

Let me stop here to make an emphatic point before we move on with the rest of the story. Jairus's daughter was dead. Jairus left home and went to Jesus because she was at the point of death. The messengers came to tell Jairus not to trouble Jesus any further, because she was dead. The professional mourners were making a great commotion at the house because she was dead. Jairus's family and friends laughed when Jesus said she was sleeping, because they knew she was dead. Jairus, his wife, and the disciples were amazed when the little girl got up and started walking around, because she was dead.

This story is a miracle because Jairus's daughter was dead. So why did Jesus say she was sleeping? He was using sleep as a euphemism for death. Jesus did not say the girl was only sleeping because she was not really dead. He called her death sleep because it wasn't permanent. It was only temporary. She wouldn't be dead for long. He was going to raise her from the dead!

The sisters, Mary and Martha of Bethany, sent a message to Jesus that their brother Lazarus was sick (John 11). When Jesus received the news that His beloved friend was sick, He remained where He was for two days. Then Jesus told His disciples, "Our friend Lazarus has fallen asleep, but I go to awaken him" (John 11:11). The disciples did not understand what Jesus was talking about. They assumed that if Lazarus was asleep, it meant he was getting better. Why make the trip if Lazarus was finally resting well? "Then Jesus told them plainly, 'Lazarus has died, and for your sake I am glad that I was not there, so that you may believe'" (John 11:14–15). For Jesus, Lazarus's death was temporary, he was only "asleep," about to be awakened by the Jesus who conquers death. The word choice "asleep" will echo His calling the young girl "asleep."

Jesus loved Lazarus. And He cared that His friend was sick. But He intentionally stayed away when Mary and Martha called on Him to intervene. And He did not arrive in Bethany until Lazarus was dead, the funeral had taken place, and his remains had been placed in a tomb. Jesus delayed His coming because He wanted His disciples to know that He has just as much power at the graveyard as He has in the sickroom. Jesus has authority at the doctor's office and the funeral home. He is in control in the emergency room and the cemetery.

This is what Jesus will show Jairus and the disciples. The fact that the girl graduated from sickness to death was not a hindrance to the power of Jesus. When doubt points to the circumstances and says it is impossible, Jesus still has the last word.

THE MOURNERS' RESPONSE TO JESUS—
AND HIS RESPONSE TO THEM

How did Jairus's neighbors and the professional mourners respond to the Lord's words of hope? "They laughed at him." (Mark 5:40). This was not a hidden chuckle. It was an open laugh of derision. They meant to embarrass Jesus. What a strange twist. These same people were just loudly weeping and wailing. But their mood abruptly changed. There was still a commotion. But it was now a commotion of ridicule rather than sorrow. They went from mourning to mocking. They knew the little girl was dead. And any suggestion otherwise was hilariously ridiculous. For the record, the unbelieving world still laughs at the notion of the power and authority of Jesus.

In response to the crowd's ridicule, Jesus "put them all outside" (Mark 5:40). This was Jairus's house. It was filled with his family and friends. But Jesus dismissed the doubters. This is when you know that Jesus is truly Lord of your life. He goes from being an invited guest to the governing host! Jesus was not angry or abusive. But He took charge of the situation. Just as He cleansed the temple of God of the money changers and dove-sellers (Mark 11:15–19), Jesus drove the doubters out of Jairus's house. Their doubt disqualified them from witnessing the miracle He was going to perform.

In Mark 6, Jesus would return to His hometown of Nazareth and be rejected by those who allowed familiarity to breed contempt. "Where did this man get these things? What is the wisdom given to him? How are such mighty works done by his hands?" they asked (Mark 6:2). "Is not this the carpenter, the son of Mary and brother of James and Joses and Judas and Simon? And are not his sisters here with us?" (Mark 6:3). They were offended by Jesus and could not believe in Him. "And he could do no mighty work there, except that he laid his hands on a few sick people and healed them" (v. 5).

Unbelief restricts the power of Jesus. No, a lack of faith does not diminish divine omnipotence. But it hinders divine willingness. Jesus deems it morally wrong to do great things where there is little faith. So He put the doubters out of Jairus's house. David Redding wrote,

> It makes us wonder what wonders might take place in the house of God now if all of those who no longer took Christ seriously were evacuated. Only a few would be left, but that is all a miracle needs. Perhaps no great things will come from the church today until this prerequisite is filled; it is hard for faith to fight for its breath in the smug and stifling atmosphere of its enemy, arrogant disbelief, or, worst of all, that treasonous saboteur, pretending faith."[2]

Having put the doubters out, Jesus led the girl's parents and His disciples into the room where the child was. He walked up to where her dead body lay and took her by the hand. Now for the third time in a short period Jesus would disregard the Jewish purity laws. In the country of the Gerasenes, Jesus met a man with an unclean spirit who dwelled among the tombs. Next, as He walked toward Jairus's home, a woman with the discharge of blood had touched Him, making Jesus ceremonially unclean. Now He touched the corpse of this little girl, rendering Jesus "unclean."

But sickness and death cannot contaminate Jesus.

So He took the girl by the hand and spoke to her. Mark wrote his Gospel from the eyewitness accounts of Peter. And he quoted the exact words Jesus said in Aramaic, "Talitha cumi." It means, "Little girl, arise" (Mark 5:41). The one who spoke to the winds and the waves (Mark 4:39) now spoke to this dead girl. Jesus invaded the realm of the dead, pointed to this little girl, and said to Death, "Give me this one back!" It was an authoritative word from a tender voice. These may have been the very words her mother used to wake her up in the morning. As if waking a sleeping child, Jesus graciously said to the dead girl, "Baby, it's time to get up now."

> **Jesus invaded the realm of the dead, pointed to this little girl, and said to Death, "Give me this one back!"**

Mark reports what happened: "And immediately the girl got up and began walking (for she was twelve years of age), and they were immediately overcome with amazement" (v. 42).

This is one of three instances in which Jesus raised the dead. Jesus raised Jairus's daughter from the dead not long after she had succumbed. Jesus raised the son of a widow in Nain (Luke 7:11–17). He stopped the funeral procession to the grave and gave the boy back to his mother. And Jesus raised Lazarus from the dead after he had been dead four days (John 11). When Jesus told them to roll the stone away from Lazarus's tomb, they warned him that the decomposed body was stinking. Yet Jesus insisted they remove the stone and spoke into the tomb, "Lazarus, come out" (John 11:43). And the dead man came back to life.

JESUS' FINAL WORD WHEN DEATH SPEAKS

These stories teach us that Jesus has the last word when death speaks. "I am the resurrection and the life," Jesus says. "Whoever believes in me, though he die, yet shall he live, and everyone who lives and believes in me shall never die" (John 11:25–26). The raising of Jairus's daughter was a proto-resurrection. It is a sneak preview of coming attractions. It points forward to the crucifixion and resurrection of the Lord Jesus Christ Himself.

Jairus and his wife were beyond themselves with ecstasy when the little girl got up and started walking around. But their daughter would die again. The son of the widow at Nain would die again. Lazarus would die again. These miracles are not recorded for us to believe in miracles. They are recorded that we would believe in Jesus. Only in His bloody cross and empty tomb is there true victory over death.

Jesus gives victory over physical death. Paul declares:

When the perishable puts on the imperishable, and the mortal puts on immortality, then shall come to pass the saying that is written: "Death is swallowed up in victory." "O death, where is your victory? O death, where is your sting?" The sting of death is sin, and the power of sin is the law. But thanks be to God, who gives us the victory through our Lord Jesus Christ" (1 Corinthians 15:54–57).

And Jesus gives victory over spiritual death. Paul said to the church at Ephesus, "And you were dead in the trespasses and sins in which you once walked, following the course of this world, following the prince of the power of the air, the spirit that is now at work in the sons of disobedience" (Ephesians 2:1–2). This is the tragedy of life without God. We are dead in our sins. "But God, being rich in mercy, because of the great love with which he loved us, even when we were dead in our trespasses, made us alive together with Christ—by grace you have been saved" (Ephesians 2:4–5).

The story ends with two commands: "And he strictly charged them that no one should know this, and told them to give her something to eat" (Mark 5:43). When Jesus set Legion free from the demons, He commanded him to go tell his family and friends how much the Lord had done for him. But Jesus most often commanded people to keep quiet about His miracles, because He did not want people following Him for the wrong reason.

> **Jesus is sovereign and sensitive . . . omnipotent and compassionate.**

In Mark chapter 1, the Gospel writer recorded a series of miracles Jesus performed. Early the next morning, Jesus went to a desolate place to pray. When His disciples found Him, they said, "Everyone is looking for you." Jesus responded, "Let us go on to the next towns, that I may preach there also, for that is why I came out" (Mark 1:37–38). Jesus did not want people to see His miracles as much as He wanted them to hear His message. Now, for this little girl, Jesus charged the parents not to tell anyone what He did for this little girl. But it was a futile command. The moment the people would see the little girl walking around they would know what Jesus did.

The second command Jesus gave was "to give her something to eat" (Mark 5:43). What a joy it must have been for that grieving mother to cook a meal for her little girl again. As she ate, it verified for her parents that their little girl was truly alive and well. Ghosts may appear to walk around. But they cannot eat!

Ultimately, Jesus gave this command for the sake of the little girl. She was raised from the dead by supernatural means. But ongoing life must still be sustained by natural means. Who knows how long this girl lay dying. She may not have eaten for days or weeks. So Jesus ordered the family to feed the hungry child.

These closing commands highlight the tension in the text between the sovereignty of Jesus and the sensitivity of Jesus. The emphasis of the text is clearly on the power of Jesus. It is the climax of a series of miracles in Mark that declares Jesus has perfect power over nature and demons and sickness and even death itself. But woven into this story of the sovereign authority of Jesus is a story about the compassionate love of Jesus.

Jesus consents to go home with this troubled father to heal his daughter. Of all the needy people in this thronging crowd, Jesus chooses to go home with Jairus. Jesus comforts this ruler when he receives the devastating news that his daughter died. Jesus risks defilement by taking the dead girl by the hand. He gently speaks to her and calls her from death to life. Then, when she rises from the dead, Jesus tells them to give her something to eat.

Jesus is sovereign and sensitive. Jesus is omnipotent and compassionate. Jesus is powerful and loving. Jesus sits high but looks low. Jesus is able and caring. And you can cast all of your cares on Him, because He cares for you (1 Peter 5:7).

And there was a woman who had had a discharge of blood for twelve years, and who had suffered much under many physicians, and had spent all that she had, and was no better but rather grew worse. She had heard the reports about Jesus and came up behind him in the crowd and touched his garment. For she said, "If I touch even his garments, I will be made well." And immediately the flow of blood dried up, and she felt in her body that she was healed of her disease. And Jesus, perceiving in himself that power had gone out from him, immediately turned about in the crowd and said, "Who touched my garments?" And his disciples said to him, "You see the crowd pressing around you, and yet you say, 'Who touched me?'" And he looked around to see who had done it. But the woman, knowing what had happened to her, came in fear and trembling and fell down before him and told him the whole truth. And he said to her, "Daughter, your faith has made you well; go in peace, and be healed of your disease."

MARK 5:25–34

CHAPTER 5

Trusting Jesus
When All Is Spent

Jesus' time with Jairus was part of another busy day for the teacher and healer. Just a few days earlier, after a long day of teaching and preaching, a tired Jesus chose to retreat from the crowds. "Let us go across to the other side," He said (Mark 4:35). In obedience to His command, the disciples set sail across the Sea of Galilee.

We know the outcome. Gale-force winds suddenly engulfed the sea. But Jesus, awakened from a deep slumber, would intervene. The Lord commanded the winds to be quiet and the waves to be still. And the unruly elements fully obeyed the voice of Jesus, to the amazement of the disciples.

After stilling the storm, Jesus and the disciples finally made it safely to land, only to encounter a demented man filled with many demons (Mark 5:1–20). Though no one had been able to tame this wild man, Jesus intervened and set him free from the unclean spirit that possessed him.

After this miraculous exorcism, the locals in this land of the Gerasenes begged Jesus to leave their country. So Jesus and the disciples crossed the sea again. When they landed this time, a heavy dose of ministry awaited.

The crowd back in Capernaum was itself large and enthusiastic. This is how it goes, isn't it? There will be people who reject you. And there will be people who receive you. And so, while the people of the Gerasenes deported Jesus, a large crowd welcomed Him at Capernaum.

FROM A RELIGIOUS OFFICIAL
TO A NO-NAME WOMAN

Here Jesus would continue to minister to those in need. Within this crowd were two people who desperately needed Jesus' help. We already have met Jairus, a ruler of the local synagogue, whose twelve-year-old daughter was at the point of death. The Lord graciously consented to go home with Jairus. But as they made their way through the crowd to Jairus's house, another desperate person interrupted them. And though she is a sympathetic character, we do not know her name. She had no apparent status. She was a nobody.

A nameless woman with a chronic disease had navigated her way through the crowd to reach out to Jesus for healing. And this is the story of her brief but powerful encounter with Jesus.

Her story is sandwiched between the story of the raising of Jairus's daughter, a parenthetical story with an important message about the difference Jesus makes. Here it is: The Lord Jesus Christ is the Great Physician who has absolute power over every disease. One of the preachers in the church of my youth would regularly pray for the sick, saying, "Lord, we know you have more healing in the hem of your garment than all the drugstores in town!" Indeed, Jesus can heal the physical diseases that afflict our bodies. And Jesus can heal the spiritual diseases that condemn our souls. This miracle over sickness demonstrates the power of Jesus over sickness of the body and the soul.

> **The ground is level at the feet of Jesus. Everyone who comes to Jesus must come the same way . . . . with childlike dependence upon Jesus.**

Still, the woman appears as an interruption, halting Jesus as He is on a mission to help a synagogue official rescue his dying daughter. The contrast between the official and the unclean woman could not be greater. Two people from different backgrounds both come to Jesus with desperate needs. One is a woman; the other is a man. Jairus is named; the woman is anonymous. He is a respected religious leader; she a shunned social outcast. He is wealthy; she is destitute. Jairus comes on his daughter's behalf; the woman comes for herself.

These two lives are as far apart as they could be. The woman is down and out. Jairus is up and in. But the ground is level at the feet of Jesus. The fact that you are somebody does not give you an advantage. The fact that you are nobody does not put you at a disadvantage. Everyone who comes to Jesus must come the same way. We must come with childlike dependence upon Jesus.

This is how Jairus and the nameless woman came to Jesus, with a desperate need that only the Lord could meet. Their stories are interwoven in Scripture. Jairus requested healing from Jesus first. But the woman received her healing first. This is the perfect timing of Jesus at work. In His infinite wisdom, it can be your time even when it's not your turn.

The healing of this woman with the discharge of blood is one of the most famous and beloved miracles of Jesus.[1] Even irreligious people are familiar with the woman with the issue of blood. And this story is understandably precious to those who believe in Jesus. In fact, Christians so love this story that unique traditions have developed around it over the centuries of church history. For instance, attempts have been made to identify this woman. The Greek Church said her name was Bernice. The Coptic and Latin Church said her name was Veronica. The historian Eusebius claimed she was a Gentile from Caesarea Philippi and that she erected a statue of Jesus in her front yard after she was healed, which became a destination for pilgrims to visit.

Of course, these are all just speculations. And, ultimately, these details are not important. What matters is what the Word of God tells us about this woman. Scripture simply tells us that this woman had a desperate condition. Yet she maintained determined confidence that brought her to Jesus. As a result of her faith, she received a divine cure that changed her life forever.

THE WOMAN'S DESPERATE CONDITION

Mark gives five details about this woman's desperate condition.

Her disease was severe. The exact nature of this woman's condition is unknown. The King James Version discreetly calls it an "issue of blood" (Mark 5:25). What does that mean? The issue of blood was a flow of blood. She was bleeding. We do not know the exact cause or nature of her bleeding. It may have been a uterine hemorrhage. Or it could have been an irregular menstrual discharge. Some internal malady caused an external flow of blood. Whatever the exact diagnosis, it was a painful, debilitating disease that drained the life from her.

Her disease was isolating. The personal ramifications of this woman's condition were bad enough. But the interpersonal ramifications were even worse. According to the law of Moses, a woman with a discharge of blood was ceremonially unclean (Leviticus 15:25–33). Everywhere she sat or slept was unclean. Anything she touched was unclean. She could not have direct contact with other people. She was barred from the place of worship. And no man could touch her (Leviticus 20:18). So this woman could not get married or have children because of her condition. Or, worse, she was married with children and her condition resulted in her being separated from them. This sick woman was a social outcast. For all practical purposes, she was a leper. She was no more welcome among the residents of Capernaum than the demon-possessed wild man, Legion, was in the country of the Gerasenes.

Her disease was chronic. The only explicit detail we are given about this discharge of blood is that it plagued the woman for twelve years (Mark 5:25). This was no passing problem. It was a chronic disease. She was dying for twelve years. Were the symptoms continual or intermittent? We do not know. Can you imagine if this was her daily experience for twelve years? She would face each new day with the torment of more painful bleeding. Facing this reality every day would have been a form of suffering that was worse than the bleeding itself. If it was an off-and-on occurrence, that would be no better. Perhaps the bleeding would stop for a few days or weeks, and her hopes would be lifted that she was finally getting better—only to have the bleeding resume. Either way, she was a living dead person for over a decade.

Her disease was incurable. This brave woman was not content to let this sickness kill her. She wanted to get better. So she went to the doctor. In fact, she visited many physicians. Mark used provocative terminology to describe her doctor visits, saying she "suffered much under many physicians" (Mark 5:26). The word "suffered" is used literally here. Her physical disease caused her to suffer. But the medical treatment caused her to suffer even more.

Believe doctors when they say they "practice" medicine. They do not and cannot perform miracles.

The Jewish Talmud describes various treatments for the discharge of blood. But these ancient remedies were nothing more than superstitious tricks. This woman visited doctor after doctor who prescribed medicine after treatment and procedure. None of it did her any good. But it certainly did help the physicians. Every doctor visit brought a new bill. Debts quickly added up. At some point, she spent whatever income and savings she had. And she could no longer afford the medical treatments. There was no such thing as insurance. And, apparently, she had no family or friends to help her.

WHEN ALL IS SPENT

Of all the things Scripture tells us about this woman's desperate condition, this sticks out to me the most. She spent all (v. 26). What an apt description of life's overwhelming circumstances. There are times when all is spent. Have you ever been there before? It is one thing not to have what you need. It is another thing to not have funds to get what you need. All is spent. Are you there now? Please, keep reading this chapter. And you will see that you can trust Jesus when all is spent.

One more thing about her desperate condition . . .

Her disease was worsening. This bleeding woman went broke seeking medical help. When all her resources were exhausted, she had nothing to show for it. Her condition did not improve. To the contrary, her condition grew worse (v. 26). The medical treatments only intensified the problem. It was like the pharmaceutical commercials that air today on American radio and TV. They offer medicine to relieve one thing. But the side effects they list are worse than the thing the medicine treats. The bold print of the magazine ads tells you the drug will change your life. Then the fine print tells you that it may kill you in the process.

Of course, these doctors did not mean to make the woman's

condition worse. They were trying to help her. But you really should believe doctors when they say they "practice" medicine. They do not and cannot perform miracles. Sometimes their treatment works. Other times, it does not. In this instance, it did not work and had unintended consequences. The physicians did all they could to help this woman. But their diagnoses were wrong. Their medicines were impotent. Their procedures were ineffective.

Luke, who was a physician himself, is more understanding in his gospel account. He claims, "She could not be healed by anyone" (Luke 8:43). But Mark is more blunt about the situation. He says the doctors took this poor woman's money and only made her condition worse (Mark 5:26). She was truly in a desperate situation.

THE WOMAN'S DETERMINED CONFIDENCE

This woman could not control what was happening to her. But she could control her response. And she chose to respond with determination. This is a distinguishing characteristic of the life of faith. Contrary to what some may teach, faith does not prevent bad things from happening in life or guarantee quick and easy resolutions to life's problems. And it does not guarantee bad things will change. Biblical faith does not give you the power to speak your desired reality into existence. But true faith can and should dictate how you respond to life's variations.

True faith maintains hope. We see this in the sick woman's determined confidence. Chronic bleeding, medical malpractice, and financial destitution could not shake her confidence. She had stubborn hope and ruthless faith that led her to Jesus.

In the crowd following Jesus, the woman reached out. She touched Jesus. "She had heard the reports about Jesus and came up behind him in the crowd and touched his garment" (Mark 5:27). When did she hear about Jesus? How did she hear about Jesus? What did she hear about Jesus? She was unclean and could not have direct contact with people. Her opportunities to hear about Jesus were limited. Yet the reports about Jesus still reached her. She heard multiple, diverse, and credible reports of the miraculous power of Jesus.

The evidence demanded a verdict. And the woman believed in Jesus. Her faith was demonstrated by what she did, not by what she said. In a word, she took a risk. When she heard Jesus had returned to Capernaum, she cloaked herself and slipped into the crowd. By stealth she pressed her way through the mass of humanity until she was right behind Jesus. Being unclean, she should not have been in that crowd. And she should not have been touching anyone. But faith moved her to take a risk. Authentic faith is not content to just know something. It does something.

So this believing woman did a simple thing for which she has been remembered throughout the centuries. She "touched his garment" (v. 27). She reached out and touched the tassel of His robe.

She trusted Jesus. Verse 27 tells us what this desperate woman did. Verse 28 tells us why she did it: "For she said, 'If I touch even his garments, I will be made well.'" Being unclean, she could not have contact with other people. So who did she say this to? Apparently, she said it to herself. There was no one else for her to talk to. And the grammar of the Greek denotes continual action. She persistently encouraged herself with the possibility of receiving Jesus' healing power.

In the ancient world, it was believed that contact with something associated with a healer could produce a miracle. It did not matter what it was, be it his clothes, a relic, or even his shadow. As a result, some Bible commentators read this woman's actions to be more superstition than faith. I disagree. The evidence is that this woman believed in Jesus. And it was real faith. Her faith in Him was so strong that it would be okay to just touch Him. And it was okay if He did not touch her. If she could just touch Him, that would be enough. No, if she could just touch the border of His clothes, she believed her healing would come. That is real faith at work!

> **If she could just touch the border of His clothes, she believed her healing would come. That is real faith at work!**

For the sake of argument, let's agree with the commentators who view her actions as superstitious faith. Assume her faith was not what it should have been. What then? I contend it would only make this miracle more remarkable. And the lesson it would teach us is that Jesus is so sensitive to our needs that He will respond to faith that doesn't have it all figured out. It doesn't matter who you are.

You may be a little child who only understands the simple facts of the gospel.

You may be a person who did not grow up in church.

You may be a seeker who is still trying to make sense of it all.

You may be an unworthy outcast who is viewed as a lost cause.

You may be a notorious sinner far from God.

But if you reach out and touch Him by faith, Jesus will respond.

THE WOMAN'S DIVINE CURE

Upon touching Jesus' garment, "immediately the flow of blood dried up, and she felt in her body that she was healed of her disease" (v. 29). Simple words to describe an incredible event. This is the third miracle in a row Mark records to demonstrate the power of Jesus. Jesus calms a storm that no one could navigate (Mark 4:35–41). Jesus delivers a demoniac that no one could tame (Mark 5:1–20). Now Jesus heals a disease that no one could cure. Jesus is the Lord of nature, the Lord of demons, and the Lord of sickness. The one who commanded storms and banished demons can also heal diseases. As the eternal Son of God, Jesus created these bodies we live in. And He is able to fix our bodies when they break down with sickness.

Jesus is able to heal sickness immediately. Verse 29 says, "And immediately the flow of blood dried up." "Immediately" is one of Mark's favorite terms, which he uses thirty-seven times. I grew up reading the King James Version, which translates the Greek word "straightway." This is how Jesus healed the woman. *Straightway. Immediately*. The cure she sought for twelve years came in an instant. What many physicians could not do happened at once. There was no recovery process. When she touched Jesus, she was immediately healed.

Jesus is able to heal sickness completely. Note the absolute reality of this miracle: "Immediately the flow of blood dried up." This statement is a metaphorical reference to the source of her condition. Whatever had caused her chronic hemorrhage immediately stopped. The sickness was healed; the need was met. She was fully restored to health. This is how Jesus works. Jesus does not treat just symptoms. He heals diseases.

The woman knew she had been restored to full health. Verse 29 says: "and she felt in her body that she was healed of her disease." It didn't matter that she could not afford to see the doctor. She did not need a doctor to verify what happened to her. She felt it. She knew it. She went from sickness to health, from weakness to strength. There was no doubt about it. She could feel the power of Jesus at work in her body. She was healed from her painful, chronic disease.

Have you got the point yet? Well, let me give it to you in plain terms. Jesus is a healer! No, I did not say Jesus was a healer. I said He *is* a healer. Is Jesus able to heal today? Absolutely! It does not matter what the sickness is. There is no such thing as an incurable disease with Jesus. He who is Lord of nature and demons is also Lord over physical sickness.

I have been a pastor all of my adult life. And in over two decades of pastoral ministry, I have prayed for countless sick people. There have been many occasions when I have prayed for the sick and God restored them to health. But there have been just as many times when I have prayed for the sick and they have died. And I had to preach the funerals of church members that I have prayed God would heal. Yet I declare that Jesus is a healer.

I was sixteen years old when my father died. As I was flying home from Detroit to Los Angeles, the Lord snatched my father from earth to glory. I have not prayed more passionately for anyone as I did for my father's healing that day. But as I prayed, I immediately sensed the answer was no. So I started to negotiate, praying that the Lord would keep him for me to get from the airport to say goodbye. That request was denied as well. But even though the Lord did not do what I wanted Him to do when I wanted Him to do it, I still declare that Jesus is a healer.

Remember, Jesus is sovereign. He is not obligated to heal in any given situation. But trust Him. Because Jesus is all-wise, he knows what's best for us when we do not. Trust Him. Because Jesus is omnipotent, when He so determines, pain, sickness, and disease are healed! Trust Him.

JESUS IS ABLE TO HEAL PHYSICAL
AND SPIRITUAL DISEASES

The healing of the woman with the issue of blood is not a guarantee of what Jesus will do in any given situation today. Divine healing is subject to sovereign discretion. God may choose to heal immediately or over time. God may choose to heal completely or partially. God may choose to heal on earth or in heaven, when we arrive with new, perfect bodies. Healing is in the Lord's hands, not ours. When sickness comes, we must trust and pray and wait on God. Either way God chooses to move, we must not make too much of physical healing.

Faith teachers claim that physical healing is the Christian's spiritual birthright. They would have you believe that the blood of Jesus gives you the authority to simply claim your healing. I wish that were so. If it were so, I would passionately declare it. But Scripture does not teach this. The truth is all of our bodies are subject to sickness that will result in death, if the Lord tarries in His coming. No exotic diet or extreme exercise routine or even living right can stop death's approach.

> **Jesus intervened. His redemptive suffering on the cross brings healing to the sin-sick soul.**

The bottom line is that we are all sin sick. Sin is painful, chronic, pervasive, debilitating, contagious, costly, and fatal. You have a date with death that cannot be canceled. But there is hope. The fact that Jesus can heal physical diseases is proof that He can heal spiritual diseases. Isaiah declared, "But he was wounded for our transgressions; he was crushed for our iniquities; upon him was the chastisement that brought us peace, and with his stripes we are healed" (Isaiah 53:5).

Healed from what? Glad you asked. Isaiah explains, "All we like sheep have gone astray; we have turned—every one—to his own way; and the Lord has laid on him the iniquity of us all" (Isaiah 53:6). We have all been poisoned by sin that will lead to eternal death. But Jesus intervened. His redemptive suffering on the cross brings healing to the sin-sick soul.

The woman with the issue of blood sneaked up to Jesus to steal a healing. And she fully expected to retreat without being noticed by anyone. But Jesus called her out to show that He is able to heal physical diseases and spiritual diseases.

"And Jesus, perceiving in himself that power had gone out from him, immediately turned about in the crowd and said, 'Who touched my garments?'" (Mark 5:30). When this woman touched Jesus, she immediately knew something happened to her. And Jesus immediately knew something happened to Him. He perceived that "power had gone out from him." This is the only place in the New Testament where this language is used of Jesus. It is a mysterious statement that raises a lot of questions. But one thing is clear. Jesus knew when this woman's faith touch accessed His divine power. He knew it beforehand. The MacArthur Study Bible notes: "Christ's 'power,' his inherent ability to minister and work supernaturally, proceeded from him under the conscious control of his sovereign will."[2]

I fully agree. Jesus did not just know what happened. He made it happen! Jesus did not ask who touched Him because He did not know. The Lord is omniscient. Nothing is "Breaking News" to the Lord of glory. He knows everything known, unknown, and knowable. Jesus asked because He wanted what He knew to be known.

When Jesus asked, "Who touched my garments?" the disciples were incredulous. With so many people trying to get to Jesus, who hadn't touched Him? Everyone was pushing and shoving to reach the Master.

The disciples were right and wrong at the same time. Many people were touching Jesus. But one person touched him not with an incidental touch but an intentional touch of faith. A woman with a chronic hemorrhage for twelve years had somehow slipped into the crowd unnoticed. She snuck up behind Jesus and touched His garment, convinced that just a touch could heal her body.

Jesus honored her simple faith. She was immediately and completely healed of her persistent disease. But Jesus would not let her slip away as quietly as she had come. He hunted her down to receive her testimony of what He had done for her. Why did Jesus flush this woman out? I propose two reasons why Jesus stopped to identify this woman.

First, Jesus stopped for the sake of the woman. She came to Jesus to receive healing for her body. But she also needed healing for her soul. She wanted physical healing. But she needed spiritual healing more than anything else. Her body was sick. But, more importantly, her soul was lost. She needed to hear Jesus say, "Daughter, your faith has made you well; go in peace, and be healed of your disease" (v. 34).

> **She came to Him trembling and fell at His feet. It was a humble posture that expressed her reverence, dependence, and submission.**

But Jesus also outed the woman for Jairus's sake. I am sure Jairus did not feel that way, as it was happening. It was just the opposite. Jairus may have been happy for the woman's healing. But he no doubt felt it was an interruption that delayed Jesus from getting to his daughter who was at the point of death. This woman had been sick for twelve years. His daughter could die at any moment. Why was Jesus wasting time? Jesus took His time to talk to the woman because He knew what was coming. He knew what was down the road. And Jesus stopped to get the woman's confession to build up Jairus's faith in advance of tragic news he would soon receive.

Hers was the intentional touch of faith. "Flesh presses," said Augustine, "faith touches." Which category do you fall in? Unfortunately, many people only bump into Jesus incidentally. Too few reach out to Him in faith to experience His transforming power. It happens in churches all the time. If the preaching or music is good, people may bump into Jesus. But how many show up with a determination to touch Jesus no matter what? Incidental contact is meaningless. But the touch of faith accesses divine power.

"The woman, knowing what had happened to her, came in fear and trembling and fell down before him and told him the whole truth" (v. 33). Picture the scene. Jesus and this woman were having a private conversation in a large crowd. He knew who He was talking to. So did the woman. She tried to get away. But the voice of the Master drew her like a magnet to Himself. She could not escape. Finally, she came to Him trembling and fell at His feet. It was the same posture Jairus took when he asked Jesus to heal his daughter (Mark 5:22). It was a humble posture that expressed her reverence, dependence, and submission.

But why did the woman come in fear and trembling? Why was she afraid? She was afraid for the same reason the disciples were afraid when Jesus made the winds be quiet and the waves be still (Mark 4:41). She was afraid for the same reason the people of the Gerasenes were afraid when they saw Legion sitting, clothed, and in his right mind (Mark 5:15). She was afraid because she knew she was in the presence of deity. This was no mere man. This was the living God.

With fear and trembling, the woman testified about her

chronic disease and divine healing. She told the whole story. The bleeding. The pain. The isolation. The doctors. The poverty. She likely went on to testify about her determination to get to Jesus and the difference Jesus made with just a touch of His garment. G. Campbell-Morgan said it well: "Contact that heals must always issue in confession that glorifies." What Jesus has performed for your good you must proclaim for His glory. You should be a witness for Jesus. Tell it to your family and friends. Let the world know the difference Jesus makes. The psalmist exhorts, "Let the redeemed of the Lord say so, whom he has redeemed from trouble" (Psalm 107:2). If the Lord has made the difference in your life, you do not have the right to remain silent.

Jesus gives personal assurance: "Daughter, your faith has made you well; go in peace, and be healed of your disease" (Mark 5:34). Scholars speculate whether this woman's name was Bernice or Veronica. But Mark does not tell us this woman's name. He instead tells us what Jesus called her: "daughter." This is the only recorded instance of Jesus addressing a woman this way. It was a term of affection. Jesus loved this woman even more than Jairus loved his little girl—with a full, unwavering, divine love.

Moreover, Jesus' words affirmed her new relationship to Him. She was more than a woman He healed. She was a daughter He adopted. This is made clear by His statement, "Daughter, your faith has made you well." She was truly healed. The verb used here is the common Greek word translated "to save" in the New Testament. It is used here to tell us that this woman was both physically healed and spiritually saved.

JESUS—NOT FAITH—
IS THE SOURCE OF OUR HEALING

What changed this woman's condition? Jesus said, "Daughter, your faith has made you well" (Mark 5:34). But let me be clear about something here. Ultimately, her faith did not make her well. Jesus did. Faith was the instrumental cause. But it was not the ultimate cause. Faith was the means. But it was not the source. Faith was the channel. But it was not the power.

There are many professing Christians today who seem to have more faith in faith than they do in Jesus. But faith is no guarantee a change will come. Jesus is. Jesus makes the difference, not faith. We see this in the series of miracles we are studying together in these chapters. The disciples' faith was weak in the storm. But Jesus rescued them anyway. Legion did not have any faith. But Jesus delivered him all the same. Jairus's faith was discouraged when the news came from his house that his daughter had died. But Jesus still went home with him and raised her from the dead.

Ultimately, it is not the size or strength of your faith that counts. It is the object of it. Faith only works when it is hooked up to Jesus. Big faith in a worthless object is futile. But just a little faith in the Lord Jesus Christ makes the difference. Jesus said to this woman, "Go in peace, and be healed of your disease" (v. 34). It was not the touch of faith that healed her. It was the authority of Jesus.

How can you know when Jesus has made the difference? You can go in peace. Peace is not the absence of trouble, conflict, or hostility. It is blessing and favor. In Jesus, we have peace with

God. Paul said, "Therefore, since we have been justified by faith, we have peace with God through our Lord Jesus Christ" (Romans 5:1). Sin makes us enemies with God. It is enmity against God. It is treason against the government of God that is a capital offense punished with eternal death. But when you trust the blood and righteousness of Christ, God declares peace.

Faith in Christ also brings the peace of God. The Lord replaces fear, anxiety, loneliness, sorrow, and emptiness with spiritual peace. Isaiah 26:3 says, "You keep him in perfect peace whose mind is stayed on you, because he trusts in you." Jesus says, "Peace I leave with you; my peace I give to you. Not as the world gives do I give to you. Let not your hearts be troubled, neither let them be afraid" (John 14:27). The apostle Paul writes: "Do not be anxious about anything, but in everything by prayer and supplication with thanksgiving let your requests be made known to God. And the peace of God, which surpasses all understanding, will guard your hearts and your minds in Christ Jesus" (Philippians 4:6–7). What a promise! When you give your situation to the Lord, you don't have to keep the peace. The peace will keep you!

You can go in peace no matter your physical condition.

You can go in peace in spite of your personal circumstances.

You can go in peace even when you receive a bad report.

You can go in peace when all is spent.

You can go in peace because Jesus makes the difference.

He went away from there and came to his hometown, and his disciples
followed him. And on the Sabbath he began to teach in the synagogue,
and many who heard him were astonished, saying, "Where did this man
get these things? What is the wisdom given to him? How are such mighty
works done by his hands? Is not this the carpenter, the son of Mary and
brother of James and Joses and Judas and Simon? And are not his sisters
here with us?" And they took offense at him. And Jesus said to them,
"A prophet is not without honor, except in his hometown and among his
relatives and in his own household." And he could do no mighty work there,
except that he laid his hands on a few sick people and healed them.
And he marveled because of their unbelief.
And he went about among the villages teaching.

MARK 6: 1-6

CHAPTER 6

The Danger of Knowing
Jesus Too Well

My father used to tell the story of a wealthy couple whose young son had a rare, life-threatening disease. As they researched treatment, they discovered the only living specialist in this area of illness lived overseas. He responded to their correspondence by claiming that he could not leave his busy practice to make the trip to the United States. You can image their disappointment in receiving this news.

In the meantime, this physician took ill under the stress and strain of his demanding responsibilities. His own doctor recommended that he take a vacation. And he chose to vacation in America, and he visited the city where this wealthy family and their sick son lived. He came to town discreetly, rented an estate, and began his own recuperation. Every day he would take a long, casual stroll down the road and back.

On one day with menacing clouds overhead, he briefed his driver as to his route and what to do if it began to rain. He walked. And it rained. So he stood on a nearby porch for shelter, waiting for his driver to rescue him. As he waited, the woman of the house noticed him. And she directed her housekeeper to get that bum off her porch. Reluctantly, he went to the door and said, "Sir, I'm sorry, but the lady of the house directed me to ask you off the porch before she calls the authorities."

Offended, the doctor complied and stood in the rain to wait for his driver to arrive. Soon the whole ordeal was over. But the doctor was so offended that he immediately packed his belongings and left the country.

The next morning, the woman of the house let out a frightening scream as she sat at her breakfast table reading the newspaper. When she was finally able to get her composure, she confessed to her husband, "The man who is able to heal our son was on our porch last night, and I turned him away."

I wonder what the response of the citizens of Nazareth was the day after the events recorded in Mark 6. Imagine the town herald standing in the gate of the city to declare the news. And the day's top story shocked the entire city: "Hometown Healer Driven Away by Unbelief." Of course, we do not and cannot know what the reaction of the people of Nazareth was when they finally realized they had rejected the long-awaited Messiah-King. Or if the people ever realized what they had done. But we do know that this rejection at Nazareth is one of the tragic incidents in the life and ministry of the Lord Jesus.

In Mark 5, a dangerous and deranged demoniac, one of the rulers of the synagogue, and a woman with an incurable disease, all express true faith in Jesus. But none of these persons who received a miracle had ever had a previous encounter with Jesus. The citizens of Nazareth, however, had an up close and personal relationship with Jesus for some thirty years. Jesus lived among them from His early childhood until the beginning of His public ministry. Yet those who seemingly knew Him the best firmly refused to put their faith in Him.

This weird paradox warns us that a false sense of intimacy with Jesus can detrimentally hinder true faith in Jesus. It can be dangerous to know Jesus too well. I know that may sound strange. But it's true. And the danger of it is that those who know Jesus too well inevitably discover they do not really know Him at all. And they miss out on the difference Jesus makes. Let the tragedy at Nazareth be a warning to you.

THE PATIENCE OF JESUS

Jesus was born in Bethlehem. But He was raised in Nazareth. He lived there until the beginning of His public ministry. And it was considered His hometown. About a year before the events of Mark 6, Jesus paid a visit to Nazareth (Luke 4:16–31). During that visit, Jesus went to the synagogue on the Sabbath day. In fact, Luke says it was Jesus' custom to attend public and corporate worship.

Visiting rabbis were typically invited to speak in the synagogue service. This Sabbath in Nazareth was no exception; Jesus was invited to speak. And the synagogue attendance may have been higher that day in anticipation of the homecoming of the new rabbi. Jesus stood up to read from the Scriptures. He chose as His text a messianic passage from the prophet Isaiah: "The Spirit of the Lord God is upon me, because the Lord has anointed me to bring good news to the poor; he has sent me to bind up the broken-hearted, to proclaim liberty to the captives, and the opening of the prison to those who are bound; to proclaim the year of the Lord's favor" (Isaiah 61:1–2).

When He finished reading, Jesus sat down and began His message. "Today this Scripture has been fulfilled in your hearing," He announced (Luke 4:21).

Initially the congregation "marveled at the gracious words that were coming from his mouth" (v. 22). But by the time He finished His message, the assembly was so shocked, angry, and offended that they took Jesus to the cliff of the city and tried to throw Him off. But Jesus passed through the midst of them unnoticed and was able to flee the scene unharmed.

Now, a year later, "He went away from there and came to his hometown, and his disciples followed him" (Mark 6:1). Feel the magnitude of this seemingly simple act. If you went to a place and the people tried to throw you off a cliff, I doubt you would go back to that place again. But a year after an angry mob tried to violently kill Him, Jesus returned to Nazareth. And Jesus did not just come to town and hide out at His family's house. He intentionally returned to the scene of the crime: "And on the Sabbath he began to teach in the synagogue" (Mark 6:2).

From a human point of view, the Lord's return to this synagogue in Nazareth was foolish, forgetful, and potentially fatal. But from heaven's point of view, the Lord's return was a wonderful expression of mercy, steadfast love, and long-suffering. Most of us would have done anything possible and everything necessary to stay away from that place, those people, and this predicament. But Jesus is the patient, persistent, and passionate hound of heaven. He went back into harm's way to give the hard-hearted people of Nazareth another chance to repent, believe, and be saved. Jesus was graciously patient with these hard-hearted people. And He continues to be patient with foolish, doubting, and rebellious sinners like you and me. Praise God!

I saw a vivid picture of grace hidden in the theology of a Dennis the Menace comic strip. Dennis was shown walking away from the Wilsons' house with his friend Joey. Both boys had their hands full of cookies. Joey then asked, "I wonder what we did to

We are beneficiaries of divine favor not because we are so good but because God is good.

deserve this?" Dennis delivered an answer packed with truth. He said, "Look Joey, Mrs. Wilson gives us cookies not because we're nice, but because she's nice."

This is our blessed reality in Christ. We are beneficiaries of divine favor not because we are so good but because God is good. "Every good gift and every perfect gift is from above," said James, "coming down from the Father of lights with whom there is no variation or shadow due to change" (James 1:17).

There is no record that Jesus ever returned to Nazareth after this episode. This fact reminds us that the God of the second chance is also the God of the last chance. But even though there is always a last chance that leads to judgment; it is always preceded by many chances to receive His grace.

Things in your life may not be as you desire. But you should be grateful that things are not as you deserve. We sometimes feel we are better than what we are getting. But you don't want God to give you what you really deserve. You should thank God that things are as well as they are. Mark it down: You are only alive and holding this book because God has been patient with you.

Peter said, "The Lord is not slow to fulfill his promises as some count slowness, but is patient toward you, not wishing that any should perish, but that all should reach repentance" (2 Peter 3:9). Many Christians believe Jesus is coming again to rapture the church, consummate the kingdom, and judge the world. The early church believed He would return during the first century. Yet multiple centuries have now passed. And Jesus is yet to return. Why the delay? It is not because Jesus makes promises He does not keep. It is because God in His mercy is seeking to give lost people time to defect from their sins, run to the cross, and trust in Jesus as their Savior and Lord.

If you have not confessed your sins to God and received His forgiveness by faith in the bloody cross and empty tomb of Jesus, you should take that step of faith today. Right now. Stop reading this book and ask Jesus to save you from the wrath to come by His atoning blood. Paul declared, "Behold, now is the favorable time; behold, now is the day of salvation" (2 Corinthians 6:2). You ought to confess your sins to God and believe that Jesus died on the cross for your sins and rose from the dead to make you right with God now.

THE PRIDE OF NAZARETH—AND OUR PRIDE

J. Oswald Sanders wrote, "Nothing is more distasteful to God than self-conceit. This first and fundamental sin in essence aims at enthroning self at the expense of God."[1] Indeed, pride is about who is going to be on the throne in your life—you or God. And when pride is in control, it hinders Jesus from working to make a difference in your life.

Pride hinders faith in the unexplainable work of God. That was the reality among the residents of Jesus' hometown. "On the Sabbath he began to teach in the synagogue, and many who heard him were astonished, saying, 'Where did this man get these things? What is the wisdom given to him? How are such mighty works done by his hands?'" (Mark 6:2). The citizens of Nazareth were astonished by the teaching ministry of Jesus. And their astonishment led to questions about the wisdom and works of Jesus. What they were hearing and seeing did not make sense to them. In their minds, they knew Jesus. He had grown up in Nazareth. He had worked as a carpenter in Nazareth for years. And his family still lived in Nazareth.

The dynamic ministry of Jesus amazed the people. And they wanted to know the source of His wisdom and power. There were only two possible options: either it was from God or it was not.

Divine power was at work through Jesus or He worked wonders by some ungodly force. What they thought they knew about

Jesus would not allow them to believe that the ministry of Jesus was from God. How could it be? He was one of them. How could He be different? "They couldn't explain him," wrote Kenneth Wuest, "so they rejected him."[2]

The Nazarenes' prideful rejection of Jesus is a stern warning to us: Do not question the credibility of Jesus based upon what you cannot understand about Him. Solomon taught, "Trust in the Lord with all your heart, and do not lean on your own understanding" (Proverbs 3:5). In other words, do not depend on what you think you know. Do not allow what you think you know to be an excuse for not trusting God. So what should you do when faith leads you beyond what you understand? "In all your ways acknowledge him, and he will make straight your paths" (Proverbs 3:6).

> **Trust that the Lord is good . . . faithful . . . all-wise, even when you cannot understand what He is up to in your life.**

Just because you cannot see what God is up to does not mean that God is not at work. Augustine said it well: "Faith is to believe what you do not see; the reward of faith is to see what you believe." True faith requires that you believe God until you see the reward of your faith: "Now faith is the assurance of things hoped for, the conviction of things not seen" (Hebrews 11:1). Faith sees the invisible. Faith believes the incredible. Faith receives the impossible. So do not question the credibility of the Lord based on what you do not understand.

Now that does not mean that you ought to stop thinking, refuse discernment, and accept everything. To the contrary, the Lord does not want you to lose your mind. We are to love God with our minds (Matthew 22:37). The Lord does not require that you check your brains at the door to believe him. But He does want to change the way you think.

The apostle Paul exhorts, "Do not be conformed to this world, but be transformed by the renewal of your mind, that by testing you may discern what is the will of God, what is good and acceptable and perfect" (Romans 12:2). Theology is faith seeking understanding. And your faith ought to seek to understand God better. But you should not doubt God because of what you do not understand. Trust that the Lord is good, sovereign, faithful, holy, and all-wise, even when you cannot understand what He is up to in your life. Charles Wesley wrote:

> Faith, mighty faith, the promises sees
> And looks to that alone
> Laughs at life's impossibilities
> And cries, "It shall be done."[3]

Pride hinders faith in the familiar work of God. In *Finding God in Unexpected Places*, Philip Yancey writes of his first visit to Old Faithful in Yellowstone National Park. Groups of tourists surrounded the geyser, their video cameras trained like weapons on the famous hole in the ground. A large digital clock stood beside the spot, predicting twenty-four minutes until the next eruption. Yancey and his wife passed the countdown in the dining room of Old Faithful Inn overlooking the geyser. When the digital clock reached one minute, they along with every other diner left their seats and rushed to the windows to see the big event. As if on signal, a crew of busboys and waiters immediately descended on the tables to refill water glasses and clear away dirty dishes. When the geyser went off, the tourists oohed and aahed and clicked the cameras; a few spontaneously applauded. But, glancing back over his shoulder, Yancey saw that not a single waiter or busboy looked out the windows.[4] Apparently, Old Faithful had lost its power to impress them.

This can happen to your faith when you think you know Jesus too well, when you have Bible knowledge and doctrine without the ongoing life of relationship and obedience He has called us to.

What the people of Nazareth saw from Jesus and thought they knew about Jesus were in conflict. It raised different questions in their hearts and minds. The questions recorded in Mark 6:2 reflect the Nazarenes' curiosity about Jesus. But the questions of verse 3 reflect their contempt for Jesus: "'Is not this the carpenter, the son of Mary and brother of James and Joses and Judas and Simon? And are not his sisters here with us?' And they took offense at him."

This verse is the only place in Scripture where Jesus is called "the carpenter." Matthew reports that Jesus was called "the carpenter's son" (Matthew 13:55). But at this point, Joseph was probably dead and Jesus had assumed his role as the local handyman. To the people of Nazareth, Jesus was just a carpenter. This was a basis of contempt for the Nazarenes. Jesus was a blue-collar worker who was handy with wood. He was not the product of any rabbinical school. Who did He think He was to teach them?

Furthermore, the citizens of Nazareth knew Jesus as the "son of Mary" (Mark 6:3). This was a derogatory slur. It was a below-the-belt blow. In the ancient Near East, children were always spoken of in relation to their father, even if their father was dead. A boy or man was always known as the son of his father. The fact that the people called Jesus Mary's son was an intentional statement about the mysterious circumstances surrounding Jesus' birth.

Then add the fact that the rest of His uterine brothers and sisters were still in Nazareth. The presence of Jesus' family in Nazareth was all the more proof that Jesus was one of them. And it also made a statement that Jesus' siblings remained in Nazareth and were not a part of the band of Jesus' disciples. These factors

> **Guard against becoming too familiar with the things of God.**

hindered the Nazarenes from putting their trust in Jesus. Simply put, they were too familiar with Jesus.

Some years ago I received a phone call from a young preacher of the church I served. He was hungry for the Scriptures and eager to preach. He called that day simply to tell me what he was learning from the text he studied. In his excitement, he remarked that he could not understand how a person could know so much about the Word of God and yet fall or remain in gross sin. I understood where he was coming from. But I felt the need to warn him that it can happen very easily. A false sense of familiarity with God's Word can dull your senses to divine truth.

Over the years of my pulpit ministry, I have tried to avoid referring to any Scripture as "familiar." You may be familiar with the wording of the text. But the truth of the Word of God is alive. My father used to say that Scripture is "pregnant." The more you study it, the more it gives birth to truth you did not see the last time you encountered the text. So we must guard against becoming too familiar with the things of God. The old axiom says that familiarity breeds contempt. But this is not the way it ought to be. And it is not the way it has to be.

"Familiarity breeds contempt," said Philips Brooks, "only with contemptible things or among contemptible people."[5] Think about it. A loving husband and wife do not think less of each other because they know each other so well. And dear friends become more intimate as the relationship deepens over the passing of years. It is all the more so with Jesus, who gets sweeter as the days go by. There may be a reason why familiarity breeds contempt with people. When you get close to them, you see their mistakes, inconsistencies, and contradictions. But not so with Jesus, who is wonderful, excellent, and beautiful in every way. Christ is an ongoing miracle. His virgin birth, righteous life, atoning death, and victorious resurrection are worthy of constant wonder, awe, and praise. Shame on us if we become familiar to the point of indifference toward the grace, goodness, and glory of the Lord Jesus!

Pride hinders faith in the ordinary work of God. Jesus responded to the recorded questions of the Nazarenes by quoting a common rabbinical proverb: "And Jesus said to them, 'A prophet is not without honor, except in his hometown and among his relatives and in his own household'" (Mark 6:4). This ancient proverb simply affirms the general point that people often neglect greatness in their midst and become easily enchanted with greatness from afar. Jerry Vines said it well: "An expert is an ordinary person who comes from another town." Yet the fact is that we often get much more excited about the person from some distant place than we do the person who is close by. Consequently, we miss what God is doing in the midst of the ordinary things, people, and means around us. In so doing we rob ourselves of many great blessings.

GOD'S OMNIPOTENCE AND ORDINARY THINGS

Here is one of the great wonders of divine omnipotence you should fully embrace and always remember: God often uses ordinary stuff to do extraordinary things!

The Lord used the ordinary dust of the earth to create man.

The Lord used an ordinary rod to help Moses perform miraculous signs and wonders before Pharaoh in Egypt.

The Lord used an ordinary boy named David to defeat the giant Goliath.

The Lord used ordinary ravens to bring Elijah bread and meat in the morning and evening.

The Lord used an ordinary lad's lunch to feed a multitude of five thousand men.

The Lord used ordinary spit, dirt, and water to open a blind man's eyes.

The Lord used two ordinary cross beams and nails to cancel your past, change your personality, and conquer your problems.

God uses ordinary things!

One day, a little boy ran a splinter into his finger. He called his father at work and cried, "I want God to take the splinter out." The father told his son that his mother could remove it easily. But that is not what the boy wanted. He claimed that it really hurt when his mom took out splinters. So he wanted God to remove it by Himself. When the dad got home an hour later, the splinter was still there. So he proceeded to remove it. And he tried to teach his son that God often uses ordinary means. God likes to use others to do His work. And sometimes it is painful.

THE POWER OF UNBELIEF

The power of faith is real, dynamic, and life changing. But while we readily acknowledge the power of faith, we often neglect the power of unbelief. However, unbelief is just as powerful as faith is. Faith honors God, so God honors faith. But the inverse of that statement is also true. Those who don't believe dishonor the Lord. So the Lord dishonors those who don't believe in Him. Remember, "without faith it is impossible to please him" (Hebrews 11:6).

We see the power of unbelief illustrated in the Lord's encounter at Nazareth. Jesus "could do no mighty work there, except that he laid his hands on a few sick people and healed them" (Mark 6:5). This is one of the most remarkable statements in the Gospels. You cannot help but be blown away by this statement if you believe that Jesus Christ is God. You see, as God became man on earth, Jesus had divine omnipotence. Omnipotence simply means that God has sovereign, perfect, and infinite power over all created things. By definition, omnipotence cannot have any limitations, restrictions, or inabilities. There just is no such thing as limited omnipotence. That is an unacceptable contradiction.

To be omnipotent means that there is nothing that you cannot do. Yet Mark, writing under divine inspiration (see 2 Timothy 3:16), dares to says that Jesus "could do no mighty work" in Nazareth. It does not say that He would not do any mighty works there. That would be easier to handle. I freely embrace the idea that Jesus only does what He wants to do. But Mark says that Jesus could not do any mighty works there. How could this be? How could Jesus be God and this text be right at the same time?

Well, let's make one thing clear.

This statement in no way indicts the divine omnipotence of Jesus. In previous chapters, we have seen dramatic demonstrations of the unlimited power of Jesus. Jesus stilled a violent storm as He and His disciples crossed the Sea of Galilee, which proves that Jesus has perfect power over nature (Mark 4:35–41). Then Jesus exorcised legions of demons from the "crazy man" in the country of the Gerasenes, which proves that Jesus has perfect power over the entire spirit world of fallen angels (Mark 5:1–20). On the way to heal the daughter of a ruler of the synagogue, Jesus healed a woman who had been chronically and incurably bleeding for twelve years, which proves that Jesus has perfect power over all sickness, diseases, and infirmities (Mark 5:24–34). Then Jesus raised the twelve-year-old daughter of Jairus from the dead, which proves that Jesus has perfect power over death itself (Mark 5:35–43).

> **The Lord did not suffer a power shortage at Nazareth. But the people there ran short on faith.**

So Jesus has perfect power over all creation. If Jesus did not have a paralysis of omnipotence, then what happened that day in Nazareth? I submit to you that the inability of Jesus to do mighty works in Nazareth had to be self-imposed. The Lord refused to permit Himself to do mighty works in Nazareth. The holy character of Jesus must have said to the divine authority of Jesus, "You cannot do mighty works here. It wouldn't be right!"

Matthew also tells the story of this tragedy at Nazareth, in which he explains why it would have been wrong for Jesus to do mighty works in his hometown (Matthew 13:53–58). Matthew reports: "And he did not do many mighty works there, because of their unbelief" (v. 58). The Lord did not suffer a power shortage at Nazareth. But the people of Nazareth ran short on faith. Blind people remained in the dark, because the city ran short on faith. Lame people remained crippled, because the city ran short on faith. The leper remained isolated, because the city ran short on faith.

Is your problem that you do not know the truth or . . . that you do not trust?

Even though Jesus has infinite power, He apparently found it morally reprehensible to bless people who don't believe. And that is still His position. A lack of faith robs you of the opportunity to experience the power of Jesus to make a difference in your life. Jesus can do what no one else can do. You can trust Him in every situation. But you must do your part. You must believe. You must put your confidence in Him. Of course, faith does not guarantee that you will get everything you want from the Lord. But a lack of faith does guarantee that you will not get much of anything from the Lord. If the Lord is going to do great things in and through your life, you must believe that He is ready, willing, and able to do it.

In the opening chapter of his book *Ruthless Trust*, Brennan Manning writes: "This book started writing itself with a remark from my spiritual director. 'Brennan, you don't need any more insights into faith,' he observed. 'You've got enough insights to last you three hundred years. The most urgent need in your life is to trust what you have received.'"[6] Can that be said of you? Is your problem that you do not know the truth? Or is it something bigger? Is your real problem that you do not trust?

I hope you have learned about Jesus from this book. I pray these chapters have caused you to think about His name, power, and identity in a fresh, new, and life-changing way. I want you to be convinced that Jesus can make the difference in your life. But I don't want you to stop there. Simply knowing about Jesus won't fix anything in your life. You must trust Him. At the airport, you have to walk the long ramp to get to the plane. And then you must step aboard.

That step is always a big step for me. When I take that first step onto the plane, I get the immediate sense that I am no longer in control. In a real sense, I wasn't in control of my life before I got on the plane. But getting on a plane makes the point loud and clear for me. Yet I don't stand there all day with one leg on the plane and one on the ramp. Neither do you, no matter how afraid you are of flying. At some point they will close the door to take off. And either you are going or staying.

Haven't you been on the ramp long enough? Now is the time to take a step of faith and trust the Lord Jesus with your situation. The knowledge of truth is useless without the presence of trust. Even demons know the truth about God and tremble (James 2:19). Spiritual knowledge accomplishes nothing if it does not lead to living faith. I hope you have learned about Jesus as you have read the chapters of this book—that Jesus is Lord over nature and demons and sickness and death. But this is not a textbook. It's a challenge. The truth about Jesus exhorts us to make a decision.

Will you just pile up more biblical information to box up and store? Or will you live out the life of the teachings of our faith?

JESUS MARVELS AT UNBELIEF . . . AND AT FAITH

The surprise of faith: "And he marveled because of their unbelief" (Mark 6:6a). This statement is just as remarkable as the previous statement about the self-imposed paralysis of the Lord's omnipotence (Mark 6:5). Think about it. Verse 5 says that the all-powerful one—He who created heaven and earth—was not able to do mighty works. Now verse 6 says that the all-knowing one marveled at their unbelief. How can one who knows everything be surprised? Again, Mark is speaking in dramatic terms to describe the severity of unbelief at Nazareth. Their hearts were so hard that Jesus was shocked, amazed, and blown away by it.

Interestingly, this is the second time Jesus "marveled" at something.

A Roman centurion had a beloved servant who was "suffering terribly" and near death (Matthew 8:6; Luke 7:2).[7] So he sent the Jewish elders of the city to ask Jesus to heal his servant. Jesus agreed. But as He approached the house, the centurion intercepted him with a message: "Lord, do not trouble yourself, for I am not worthy to have you come under my roof. Therefore I did not presume to come to you. But say the word, and let my servant be healed" (Luke 7:6b–7). When Jesus heard these words, "he marveled at him, and turning to the crowd that followed him, said, 'I tell you, not even in Israel have I found such faith" (v. 9).

This centurion, a ranking officer in the imperial army of Israel's oppressors, demonstrated faith in Jesus that exceeded anything the Lord had seen from anyone else in Israel. And the fact that such great faith was demonstrated where you would least expect it surprised Jesus. But at Nazareth Jesus was surprised that such unbelief was being demonstrated where one would expect there to be faith (Mark 6:6).

Let me ask you a question. Is the Lord surprised at your faith? Or is He surprised at your unbelief?

My final challenge to you, dear reader, is attempt great things for God and expect great things from God. Tell the Lord, "I believe; help my unbelief!" (Mark 9:24).

Notes

Chapter 1: Embracing the Priorities of Jesus

1. Warren Wiersbe, *Be Diligent* (Colorado Springs: Cook, 2010), 33.

2. R.C Sproul, *Now That's a Good Question* (Carol Stream, IL: Tyndale, 1996), 260–61.

Chapter 2: Trusting Jesus in a Storm

1. Amy Carmichael, *Edges of His Ways* (Fort Washington, PA: CLC, 1995), October 6. In public domain.

2. This miracle of Jesus is also recorded in Matthew 8:23–27 and Luke 8:22–25.

3. Philip Yancey, *Finding God in Unexpected Places*, rev. ed. (New York: Random House, 1995; Colorado Springs, Waterbrook, 2008), 218.

4. John F. MacArthur Jr., *The MacArthur Study Bible* (Nashville: Nelson, 2007), 1432.

Chapter 3: Trusting Jesus to Set You Free

1. This miracle of Jesus is also recorded in Matthew 8:28–34 and Luke 8:26–39.

2. David A. Redding, *The Miracles of Jesus* (Old Tappan, NJ: Revell, 1971), 143.

3. C. S. Lewis, *Surprised by Joy*, (New York: Houghton Miffin, 1966), 226.

4. Lawrence Richards, *The Bible Readers Companion* (Wheaton: David C. Cook, 2002), 637.

Chapter 4: Trusting Jesus at a Dead End

1. Harry A. Ironside, *Expository Notes on the Gospel of Mark* (Neptune, NJ: Loizeaux Brothers, 1982), 83.

2. David A. Redding, *The Miracles of Jesus* (Old Tappan, NJ: Revell, 1971), 157.

Chapter 5: Trusting Jesus When All Is Spent

1. This miracle of Jesus is also recorded in Matthew 9:20–22 and Luke 8:43–48.

2. John F. MacArthur Jr., *The MacArthur Study Bible* (Nashville: Nelson, 2007), 1433.

Chapter 6: The Danger of Knowing Jesus Too Well

1. J. Oswald Sanders. *Spiritual Leadership* (Chicago: Moody, 1980), 226.

2. Kenneth Wuest, *Word Studies in the Greek New Testament*, vol.1 (Grand Rapids: Eerdmans,1950), 121.

3. Charles Wesley, "Father of Jesus Christ, My Lord," verse 3, *Hymns and Sacred Poems*, 1742; in The Methodist Hymnal (New York: The Methodist Book Concern, 1905), 297. In public domain.

4. Philip Yancey, *Finding God in Unexpected Places*, rev. ed. (New York: Random House, 1995; Colorado Springs, Waterbrook, 2008), 218–19.

5. As quoted in Roy B. Zuck, *The Speaker's Quote Book* (Grand Rapids: Kregel, 2009), 189.

6. Brennan Manning, *Ruthless Truth* (New York: Harper Collins, 2000), 1.

7. See Matthew 8:5–13 and Luke 7:1–10 for the full account.

Acknowledgments

I would like to thank those who have assisted me in getting this book into your hands.

It has been a joy to work again with Moody Publishers, who partnered with me in publishing my first two books. Thanks to Karen Waddles for helping to open this door. Special thanks to Roslyn Jordan for keeping the project on track. And thanks to Jim Vincent for his expert editorial work.

I also owe a debt of gratitude to those who have taught me. There are some who have taught me by their teaching, example, and mentorship. Others have taught me by their writings. The strengths of this book exist because of those who have invested in me. The weaknesses are all mine.

I praise God for the Shiloh Metropolitan Baptist Church. This work began as a series of messages at our midweek worship service, which our members warmly received. I cannot express how blessed I am to serve such a wonderful congregation.

A big shout-out goes to the Shiloh Church staff. Because of

your hard work I am free to study, teach, and write. In particular, I am grateful for service of my executive assistant, Nicole Clark, who is the reason I make any deadline. Thank you all for your partnership in the gospel.

I have dedicated this book to my wife, Crystal; whose care for me and our family make ministry possible.

Our three terrorists . . . uh, I mean children, are the best! Thanks, H.B. III, Natalie Marie, and Hailey Breanne for sharing your old man. I love you and am so proud of the people you are becoming!

Above all, I give all praise to the Lord Jesus Christ who has made the difference in my life!

It Happens After Prayer

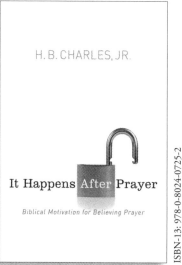

Whatever the obstacle in your path. Whatever it is that you have tried to move without success. You have not done enough or used all your strength if you have not asked God for help and prayed about it sincerely, diligently, and persistently. In *It Happens After Prayer*, Pastor H. B. Charles, Jr. encourages you to consider your prayer life and know that whatever your need or situation, prayer is the place to begin. You can pray to God with confidence, trusting that He hears and will answer.

Also available as an ebook

MOODY
Publishers™

*From the Word **to** Life*

www.MoodyPublishers.com

ON PREACHING

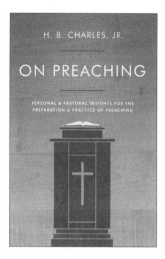

978-0-8024-1191-4

Being a preacher comes with great privilege and awesome responsibility. It is a humbling task that calls for laying spiritual, mental, and physical groundwork. Whether you are just starting to preach or have been preaching for some time, in *On Preaching* H.B. Charles seeks to encourage, as well as challenge and motivate you through personal and pastoral insights he's learned over the years. These insights will help you improve on your preparation process and ungird your efforts to be an effective preacher.

Also available as an ebook

MOODY Publishers™

From the Word to Life

www.MoodyPublishers.com

urbanpraise

Urban Praise, a commercial-free Moody Radio Internet station, offers a soulful blend of rich gospel and urban music. Energize your faith with artists like Kirk Franklin, Israel Houghton, Shirley Caesar, CeCe Winans, Walter Hawkins, and Lecrae, along with bite-size teaching segments from Tony Evans, Crawford Loritts, Melvin Banks, Beth Moore, and others.

www.urbanpraiseradio.org

MOODY
Radio™

*From the Word **to Life***